The Secret To Blended Families Marriage and Parenting Success

Making Peace, Escaping the Drama, and Successfully Solving Marriage and Parenting Problems in the Blended Family

By Daren Carstens

Carwayne Publishing

ISBN-13: 978-0989371605 (Carwayne)

ISBN-10: 0989371603

Cover Designer: Adam Carstens

Digital Book(s) (epub) produced by Carwayne Publishing

Why You Need To Read This Book

Whether you have children that are a product of a divorce, death, or another life-changing experience, adding a new set of siblings and parents into the mix can be a traumatic event, no matter how pleasantly it goes. When an adult decides to move on and take that fateful step into marriage once again, the families that result from that marriage can be quite a combo. In this book, Daren Carstens, along with his wife, will give you advice, ideas and theories that will help you along this new road that you are travelling. You will learn how to love your spouse more; how to properly discipline your biological children and stepchildren; how to create a fun, loving household; and how to move on by grasping the joy that each day in a blended family provides. With their help, you will realize that things that may seem like curses can be turned into amazing blessings. Life is precious, and learning how to live a peaceful one inside of a house full of different personalities is something to be treasured. This book will help you do just that.

Are you part of a blended family? Have you been struggling to make everyone in your home feel special and equal? From stepbrothers and stepsisters to live-in grandparents and adopted children, blending a family is a long and complicated process. With the help of Daren Carstens and his wife Laura, you will walk through a step-by-step process and be led into a peaceful, productive marriage, family life, and personal life. Are you divorced? Have you adopted a child? Or has Grandma moved in to the spare bedroom? All of these things are examples of the components that make up the different parts of a blended family, and what can make the transition into a cohesive unit so difficult.

This book will help you manage your marriage, whether it is a new marriage, or a marriage after a divorce or death, in which you are blending two previous families into one. You will get tips of the trade from an experienced family, as well as the inspiration that it takes to help you create a foundation that will withstand any storm.

By reading this book, you will gain the tools that you need to deal with strife, rebellion, and disagreements. Those tools will help you to build a strong family that lives a fun, peaceful life. Packed full of quotes and stories, this book will also help you ease your stress over your new situation, reduce bickering within your family, and handle the personal trauma that every person in the family unit goes through after a big change. You will also learn how to regain your love for each other, recover your passions in life, and how to explore those passions as a family set to tackle the world together.

Throughout this book, we will explore how to handle the tensions between new siblings by teaching brothers and sisters how to become lifelong friends. Daren explores different theories on how to stop jealousy between siblings, how to assure that everyone in the household feels special, and how to create ways to celebrate each other on a daily basis. You will learn how to deal with marital disagreements, and how the way you deal with those disagreements affect the rest of your family. You will gain insight into why your behavior is so important to the rest of the family, and you'll learn how to decide whether or not you need more help in your blended family.

If a friend of yours is dealing with this situation, then this book is the perfect gift. If you are in a blended family or you have a family member who is in this situation, the advice and leadership that Daren and Laura will give you will prove to be an invaluable gift. Share this book with your spouse and work together as the heads of your family to bring everyone closer. You will learn to give each other the support that both of you need as husband and wife, and through that, your children will learn to support each other.

After you have used all of these wonderful tools, please be sure to review this book so that others can gain insight into how they may be inspired by it.

Personal Note from the Author

This book blends 24 years of blended family experience and pastoral experience as a man who has personally gone through a divorce and remarriage. I am a pastor who has worked with and counseled many couples concerning marriage, relationships, and parenting. I know the emotions concerning the blended family and the difficulties in marriage for those in a blended family. I used to second-guess, question, and doubt myself as my wife and I dealt with the difficulties of ex-spouses, finances, child support, parenting, discipline, differences of opinion, and well... that list could go on and on. At many times, my wife and I felt like we were failing.

That is why we put together this marriage and parenting guide to success. It will bring healing and peace, and will let you see that there is hope and a future for your family. This book will help you regain your sense of control and confidence as a member of an extra-special type of family. My intention is to give you the help you need to have a successful and peaceful marriage in an emotionally safe home.

Daren Carstens

INTRODUCTION

NO Unnecessary Roughness

Let's face it: marriage can be rough. In fact, it can be *extremely* rough! Mix in some ex-spouses, stepchildren, step-siblings, in-laws, finances, expectations, discipline, sexuality, and shake it all up until you have a blended family. Wow! It can be exhausting. That is where this book comes into play. Let's go from being exhausted to getting excited about how lucky that we are to be a part of such a unique set of circumstances.

Within the pages of this book, I am going to bring you much hope along with some very practical solutions to help you navigate and negotiate the sometimes vicious and rough day-to-day life of a blended family. You will be encouraged, your guilt and shame will be lifted, and hope and peace will enter your home as you realize that you are not alone. There is a way to have a peaceful family. It not only *can* but it *will* get better.

My name is Daren Carstens, and like so many of you, I have been through a divorce. I am now a pastor, dad, husband, friend, and mentor to many who are seeking hope and encouragement. My goal is to bring you help. This book is about bringing a message of encouragement to you and your family. You can have better days. My prayer for you as we begin this wonderful journey of practical healing and help is that all your pain, hurt, discouragement, guilt, and shame be lifted from your heart and soul.

If you feel overwhelmed in your blended family, many times it is because you don't know where to start, because the task of dealing with our pain, hurt, and issues may seem so complex and daunting that we never get started.

In the next 24 hours, 3,000 couples will split up. Of the 35% of those who try to stick it out, 75% say they feel like they are in deep weeds. 10% report that they are absolutely miserable. 65% of all marriages end up in divorce. More than half of new marriages this year will not make it. This book isn't going to tell you how to save those marriages. It's going to tell you how to move on and pick up the pieces once the drama has come to an end. Forgive yourself, forgive others, and live the life that God intended you to live.

When I looked for some established Christian programs or guidelines dealing with today's definitions of family and the issues of blending, I discovered that churches have either attempted to approach the subject from a distance, or they have stayed clear altogether. But I believe that together with God, we have the potential to develop some of the best teachings on the subject of family and marriage that have ever been made available.

Divorce is the number one cause of blended families, but it's not the only one. Death and adoption also contribute. If we include bi-racial and multi-generational families, then we expand the group even more. If you are single and want to marry someone with children, then this information is important to you, too. The possibilities are endless. No matter what your status is right now, you will find that you fit into one of the situations we will talk about. No matter what your background is or where you are in your journey, God wants to touch your life.

Is it going to be easy? No. Blending families is tough because there are so many factors that come into play. Just a few possible conflicts that we will discuss are listed below. Trust me, I know that there are more, but the same methods of love and biblical foundations can be used throughout most situations.

- *Biological vs. Step children*
- *Ex-spouses and New spouses*
- *Ex-husband's new wife, or ex-wife's new husband*
- *His kids / Her kids / Our kids*
- *Parenting styles*

- *Custody*
- *Discipline – What's fair? What if we don't agree?*
- *Fighting fair*
- *Loyalty*
- *Guilt – how a split affects children*
- *Confrontation – children, step-children, ex-spouses*
- *Lawyers*
- *Past sins of a father or mother*
- *Overcoming mistakes*
- *Helping children heal*
- *Reducing stress*
- *Clarifying core values and establishing priorities*
- *Money*

Bitter or Better?

When a home falls apart, our dreams, goals, vision, and hope can be left crushed and broken. Our lives are turned upside down. The past is buried in the rubble. We don't know who to trust any more. We're not sure how to move forward. Isn't every child's worst nightmare that Mom and Dad will get a divorce? For many, the nightmare becomes real. There is so much to do that everyone in the situation often feels overwhelmed and broken. When we go through tragedy, when we go through hurt, when we go through betrayal, we are faced with a decision, a choice. We can either get bitter from it, or we can get better from it.

Working through the pain and brokenness can help us move from hatred back to love, and ultimately, to forgiveness. How do I know that? Long before I became a pastor, I went through a divorce. I've walked through the fire with my own family. We are blended. **Much of who I am as a person, a pastor, a husband, and a dad is a result of allowing God to take the brokenness of my past and create something even better.**

My Story

When I was 19 years old, I married my high school sweetheart, the homecoming queen. At that time in my life, I didn't know what to look for in a mate. I didn't even know what kind of mate I could be, and I didn't care. We were nothing alike. We were not compatible at all. But opposites attract, right? So I went against the advice of my dad and got married anyway. Long story short – I was an idiot.

Because of my beliefs about marriage, I was committed to trying to make it work. I didn't leave. Five years in, the marriage was horrible. There was no friendship and we had no common interests. Our only common ground was our two little girls. Her constant threats of leaving kept me on an emotional rollercoaster. Then one day I came home from work and walked into an empty house. It was the weirdest feeling. And **as painful as it was, it was as if the weight of the world had been lifted off my shoulders.**

I learned a lot from this experience. Although opposites attract, they can have completely different expectations about just about everything. It's hard to make important decisions together when you don't see eye to eye. Like many young couples, I thought that after we got married, I could bring her around to my way of thinking. FORGET IT! You can't change another person.

It's important to take a good look at the practical aspects of marriage, as well as the romantic, before tying the knot. Sexual attraction is important, but it's only a small part of life. If you're not compatible, the attraction will dwindle quickly, and then you will be left with emptiness. If you want to get some idea of how your partner will deal with the daily issues of life, take a look at his or her parents' relationship. We unconsciously embody what we see our parents do. If your spouse has had modeling that teaches running away from hard times, guess who could be left standing? There's much to consider.

When I met Laura, my wife, she was single. She had never been married and didn't have any children. The closer we got, the more she loved my girls. It was incredible! But this is where the real work started. Faith is a compass, not a stopwatch. In other words, our faith points us in the right direction, whereas a stopwatch puts a starting time and ending time to our progress. And your faith is what it will take for you to get through things. Without it, you may as well not even begin to try and understand why you are where you are and what you are going to do next.

I wish I could say that after 23 years of marriage, everything is perfect. I wish I could tell you that we never have disagreements, that we never get upset, or that we never raise our voices. I wish I could say that we just sit with our feet propped up on the coffee table eating chocolates and drinking coffee all night long. Nice fantasy! In reality, it's the awareness that grows from each new challenge, and the closeness that we feel after rising up to meet it that becomes the gift. After all, it's the journey, not the destination.

Proverbs 13:17 – *"Reliable communication permits progress."*

A woman went into an art shop, seeing a painting that caught her eye. When she got inside, she saw about 50 beautifully framed prints priced at $25. Then she saw another painting, similar to the prints, but slightly different. It was a little rougher, had a few smudges, and had no frame. It was just a stretched canvas with frayed edges. Thinking of the $25 framed prints, the woman imagined that this would cost less. When she turned it over, she saw a $2000 price tag. Thinking there was a mistake, she asked the clerk about it. The clerk told her that this was an original. The master artist had touched this one with his own hands. The others had their smudges and imperfections airbrushed out. But this was the original, as painted by the artist. What made it so valuable were the smudges and imperfections, exactly as he created them.

There have been so many days that I have wished that I could airbrush out the imperfections on the canvas of my life, that I could paint over my mistakes and failures and airbrush out my weakness, faults, and shortcomings. But I was made in the image of the Master Artist. I am valued just as I am. I have been touched by Christ. I am a masterpiece. YOU are a masterpiece, no matter where you've been bruised, who you've scratched, or where you have failed. God has a plan for you and the family that you are raising by his guidelines. Now it's up to you to trust Him.

Romans 9:17 – *"I raised you up for this very purpose, that I might display my power in you and that my name might be proclaimed in all the earth."*

Philippians 4:12-13 – *"I know what it is to be in need, and I know what it is to have plenty. I have learned the secret of being content in any and every situation, whether well fed or hungry, whether living in plenty of in want. I can do everything through him who gives me strength."*

Table of Contents

CHAPTER 1

ONE Recipe for a Sweet Marriage (icing optional)

Can We Have a Sweet Marriage?

Blending a family is a lot like creating a recipe. Individual ingredients can be very tasty   as long as we keep them separate. It's when we blend them together, that they can become gross and bitter. Bringing a family together can cause a similar dynamic.

Typically, we have a bunch of really good people, with good intention, in blended families, who have become comfortable with things the way they are. When people are taken out of their comfort zones, it can make them uneasy and uncomfortable; at first. It requires us all to change a little, and that can be scary. Fear can bring out our issues. You've heard the expression, 'the devil we know is better than the devil we don't know.'

Resistance to change doesn't just occur in this type of blended family. If we talk to people, we discover that actually every family is blended. Anytime two people come together we have a blend. We come from different backgrounds and have different ways of doing things. Some children are athletes and some are artistic. We are blending individuals and families, including in-laws and outlaws alike. We're bringing the whole group together. It's a whole lot like taking a drink out of that superfood smoothie that is supposed to be so healthy for you. You know that it's for the best, but it can leave a very unusual taste in your mouth.

So once if you are in the situation where you are starting over, you will need a foundation, a recipe for success, a how-to guide that lays out the building blocks of a marriage and the love within it.

Laura and I desire to attempt something here that, as far as we know, has never been done before. We want to open the door and give you a glimpse of what it's like at our house.

As we work through our experience of blending, we want to share what it's like from both sides of the issues. We hope it will bring you many insights and answers.

I want to give you a key truth, which is foundational to this whole blended family concept. In order for everything to work, we really have to understand and apply this truth. *All of us have different definitions for different words.* Your idea about the meaning of a particular word may differ from mine. When we talk about relationships, marriages, or families coming together, we all have different ideas of what we think they should be. We all have different pictures in our mind of what things look like. But the most important definition of the way a family should work and look is God's.

When you talk about God and the nature of God, the first thing that comes to mind is the unconditional love of the Father. Throughout the Bible, God compares His love for us, his people, to a relationship called marriage. Unconditional love is the first thing He talks about. There are different levels of love and different scriptural words defining these levels. The first Bible term is called 'agape' love. If you've been around church very long, you know that agape is a hip church word. Agape love is God-like, unconditional love. Agape love is initiative taking love. This kind of love initiates love. It is also a commitment to making love work. *This type of love has to be the very foundation for all of our relationships.*

Built in the early 1920s and perched on the bluffs of the Mississippi River in Alton, Illinois is the Olin Mansion. If you've ever been inside this historical landmark and gone into the basement you will see the foundation of that great structure. You'll notice that there are no cracks, not one. This thirty-six thousand square foot house is over 75 years old. So much time, energy and money were contributed to the building of its rock solid foundation that to this day every door swings perfectly. Why? The foundation has never moved. It hasn't shaken. It hasn't shifted. It hasn't cracked. It is as solid today as it was when it was built because it's built upon a good foundation.

Agape love, the unconditional love initiated by God is the solid rock that can withstand time. This must be the foundation of every relationship, whether it's for the children, wife, husband, or anyone else. For the success of our relationships, we should all commit this type of unconditional love. This commitment loving unconditionally, will build a true and lasting foundation for the relationship to grow and blossom into the mature relationship that God has made possible for us to have.

Let's build. The next level of the love foundation is called Phileo love. The Bible calls Phileo love a friendship type of love. It's the warm friendly love existing between best friends. There are certain people in your life you get close to and develop this kind of love for. You have friends that you have warm, fuzzy feelings for. It feels good. This is a good place to start a relationship. Start out as friends. It's the old age idea of courting that can get you to this place. Do things together that require you to talk about your likes and dislikes, pet peeves and dreams.

The next form of love is called Eros love. This is where we get the word 'erotic' or 'erotica.' This is the sexual attraction side of love. It's the physical, the turn on, the hormones and the sex drive. Can we talk about that in a Christian book? Here's the problem; we haven't talked about it. It needs to be discussed. Christians, by and large, avoid this subject. But God created us with a sex drive. He hard wired us with the drive to procreate. He also provided us with a guidance system to help us control our choices. He wants us to experience, enjoy, and talk about all of the loves that he has blessed us with.

The next level of love is called Hasid. Hasid love is the 'favor' type of love. It's the kind of love that does special things. This is what God says He has for His people. It's expressed through loyalty. It's the type of love you only experience with a handful of people in your life. Hasid love is the kind of love you can call upon at three o'clock in the morning, no questions asked. If you say, *"Get down here right now and bring one hundred dollars with you. I need it now."* And the answer is, *"I'll be right there."* Now how many of those friends do you have? These are friends that have your back, good or bad. They just don't have your back when you're doing everything right. They're with you when you're all messed up and making bad decisions. They are saying, *"You're all messed up man, but I still love you. I'm with you."* We all need those kinds of friends. The Bible says that God is that way with us. He has the Hasid type love for us. He extends favor, grace and mercy toward us. He even draws us in when we are messed up. Why? He has Hasid love toward us. And if we are the image of God, then we should have this kind of love for everyone, especially our spouse.

Now that we've introduced the various types of Biblical love, let's take a look at how they fit together. Agape is the foundation of love that all the others are built upon. The world gets the foundations of love mixed up when trying to build healthy relationships. The world often tries to build relationships on the Eros type of love. It's like laying concrete. If you just pour the dry mortar down on the ground it is just a powder that can be blown away and absorbed into the ground. You need to add the other components, like rebar and water in order to form the mixture that then turns into rock. One component alone may seem to be enough, but eventually it withers away. Solidarity will form if you use all the types love together to form your rock.

The world often says, *"Hey, he's a good looking guy, that's good enough for me."* Or *"Wow, she's really hot, I want her."*

If you choose a mate this way, then it is highly likely that you will make some bad choices. You are only as pretty as your first argument. Beauty goes out the window when you are in intense fellowship with one another. If you've ever been around a beautiful woman who has a mean-spirited personality, then you know how quickly she loses her "beautiful". The same can go for a man, but we typically don't judge guys on beauty. In today's culture, guys are judged less for their looks than a woman is. When women describe men, they generally describe traits; he's gentle, kind, honest and a hard worker. When men describe women, they usually refer to physical attributes.

Ephesians 5:31-32 NKJV *"For this reason a man shall leave his father and mother and be joined to his wife, and the two shall become one flesh." This is a great mystery, but I speak concerning Christ and the church."*

The reason I quoted this scripture is because throughout the Bible there are numerous references to the relationship between a husband and wife in the confines of marriage as it relates to Christ and the church. It's a mystery. Marriages outside of the covenant, those who have not accepted Christ as their Savior as of yet, can only build a marriage relationship on Phileo (best friend) type love, Eros (erotic) type love or some Hasid (friends to the end) type love. If they don't have Agape type love, which is God type love, they really don't have the full picture or mixture of what a loving relationship should be. To be perfectly honest, they are missing out.

Now let's go a step further. A Christian couple can miss the element of Agape type love in their relationship as well by simply not applying it. They may not truly understand this type of love. That's why the Bible refers to it as a mystery. But in heaven, Paul explains, the mysteries are made clear to those who are in covenant with Christ. This is why it is vital to the health of their marriage to be in an intimate, growing relationship with Christ.

I want to help you deal with ex-wives and ex-husbands. I want to help you deal with conflict. My two biggest family struggles involve my biological children, who don't live with me. They didn't grow up with me. I only had them with me every other weekend. There were a number of things that were more comfortable for me to avoid because I only saw them four days a month. They lived an hour away from me. The separation made it easy for me to avoid a lot. Here's my point. Love is a decision.

Decisions, Decisions...

Love is about decision making. We often mess this up. We think love is about emotions and feelings. But love is a decision. I agree there has to be a little bit of Eros attraction or it has to develop over time – you do want to get married to someone that you're attracted to. But there is a much greater foundation than attraction. At some point in the relationship, you have to make the decision. It's a choice.

In the weddings I perform, I always ask, "*Do you choose this woman?*" And I ask the bride, "*Do you choose this man?*" Why do I ask this? Because it is a decision; it is a choice. You have a *choice.*

This morning, when I got up to get dressed, I didn't just walk into my closet and wiggle around and come out dressed. I walked into the closet, looked around, and evaluated what I wanted to wear. I had to choose what to put on. I made a choice. I like what the Bible says here:
Colossians 3:14 NKJV *But above all these things put on love, which is the bond of perfection.*

What Paul tells us here is that the key to making everything else work in our lives is to put the love on. Get dressed in love. When you get up in the morning, you make a decision to put love on. You decide you are going to carry unconditional love and wear it all day long, no matter who crosses your path.

Lust comes and goes. It has cycles. Sexual feelings are fragile and fickle. Looks change. Preferences change. Have you ever noticed that the older some people get, the better they look? I went to a high school reunion recently. I saw people I went to school with and if I didn't know them, I would guess some of them to be twenty years older than I am. We change. My wife gets prettier every year. That's cool. Her looks never fade. Mine do. That is how God sees us.

Listen, we all age. We all grow older. The beauty we have in our youth does not stay with us forever. If your decisions are based upon looks or appearance, what do we do when those things change? Are we so fickle that the relationship falls apart when looks change? It shouldn't be that way. There ought to be a commitment there. Circumstances change, too.

Behave Yourself!
Love is all about behavior.

John 14:15 NIV *"If you love me, you'll obey what I've commanded."*

Love has certain behaviors and activities that are part of it. Love is about being committed. This is more of the Agape type love. There comes a time in every relationship when that commitment is tested. In a blended family, or in any family, it's tough to navigate the often turbulent waters of blending. To navigate those rapids, you have to be committed. Strap yourself in and conquer the rapids, because the calm view at the end of the river is totally worth the fight.
My wife and I talked about this before we got married. One of the reasons we discussed this was because of my experience in my first marriage. I did not want to get into a relationship and hear, "Well, let's just get a divorce." I never want to hear those words again.

Laura and I agree with these statements and use them as building blocks and structure in our marriage:
"I will love you forever. I will stay committed to you forever."

"You will never have to worry about me threatening to divorce you or leave you. No matter how bad it gets, I won't leave. I will be married to you, even if we are miserable. You may choose to leave but I will not."

"I will not try to change you or make you any different. I love you the way you are."

Our marriage is based on these agreements and a Christ-centered life. God is the foundation of our marriage. Because of Agape and Phileo (friendship type) love, I'm not trying to change her, and she's not trying to change me. We work on ourselves with God. And somehow the Eros type of love just shows up anyways. It's crazy how God makes that work.

Sometimes we want to change. We want to do the right things. The person who frustrates me more than anybody is *me*. I'm my own worst enemy. I frustrate myself more than anybody in my family can. The other day Laura asked me, *"Are you alright?"* I replied, *"I'm just really frustrated with myself."* I had misplaced something that I was looking for. It was getting to me. It happens that way sometimes.

When you're frustrated with yourself, you can bring those feelings to God. God can help you – humble you. But when your spouse tries to humble you, you become defensive. Then the walls go up. Once you put the walls of defense up, then it is difficult to change. You won't change. I'm convinced that the worse thing we can do is try to change other people.

I'm a pastor of a growing church. If I started trying to change the members of my church every Sunday morning, then it would not be a growing church. I would stunt its growth. If my sermons were filled with you should, you ought to, you must, you have to, or if I started my sermons addressing all of our sins – I'd have no members and no readers. The ones who stick around simply because they love me would be miserable.

First of all, I should never try to change you because that's between you and the Holy Spirit. My job is to love you unconditionally and to teach you the Word. Yes, the scripture does say, "...*correct, rebuke and instruct...*" but I do that through the Word. Then the Holy Spirit does the changing in you. And the change He will make in you is breathtaking; if you let him.

Sometimes I sit with my sons or my daughter as a father and I correct them, rebuke them, or instruct them. Sometimes I'm frustrated and a little bit wound up, but I do it in a spirit and a heart of love for them. I want the best for them. This type of commitment is the cold steel commitment of love.

I am a *Divorcee*

If you have gone through the pain of a divorce, my heart goes out to you. I know how hard and how painful a broken relationship is. My goal in this writing is not to bring any kind of finger pointing or blaming or even any condemnation to you for the cause of your divorce. Whether you are the victim of a divorce, the one who initiated the split, or were the cause of divorce, I have good news for you! Help is here. This isn't the blame game. That divorce is over. You are moving on and getting ready to blend a new family and that is why you are reading this book. So this next section isn't about anything that happened in the past, it is about your future and how to keep it from happening again.

Malachi 2:16 "*I hate divorce.*"

God is saying, "*I hate divorce.*" Do you know the reason He hates divorce? One reason is because He loves us so much. The second reason is He knows that things can be healed, and things can be restored. So often the reason a marriage falls apart is because one of the two parties throws in the towel and takes a walk. The marriage could have worked. It could have been restored if two people would have applied themselves. It takes two people working at it. One can have a totally pure heart, in the game, ready to work at it, but if one bolts, it's over. Remember, you can't control another human being. Do you know there is a great peace and security that comes from not trying to make someone love you? You can't do it. Another reason God hates divorce is because we can all be healed. When you divorce, if you choose to walk, you're in deep trouble with God. Some say the grass is greener on the other side of the fence. That's also where the cow dung is. You think you're going to greener pastures but end up standing in poop. It stinks. It's nasty. The others in the pasture need healing, too. The church is also responsible for those souls. We all need some help to get cleaned up. We all make mistakes and need to feel welcomed. We all need love. 'All' leaves nobody out.

Janice Abram Spring wrote, *"Most people wait for love to return before they recommit to their marriage."* I say just the opposite. The couple has to recommit to the marriage before feelings of love return. Many people are waiting for the feeling of love to come back to their marriage. The feelings aren't there. The passion isn't there. When you notch the commitment up and you recommit to the institution of your marriage, then the feelings will eventually return to you. When you begin to put that other person first in your marriage, God will honor that and He will touch you.

I remember twisting my ankle once. It was really bad. The tendon snapped. I was playing basketball with a group of guys, and I came down on the wrong side of my ankle. It was the most pain I'd ever had in my life. It was horrible. I went to the doctor for some pain pills. I took one and didn't feel any relief. I took another and started feeling a little bit of relief. I took three of the pain killers and guess what? I was under the influence of drugs – really bad. Under the influence of three pain killers, I laid down on the couch in my living room. I have vivid memories of blank periods of times. I vaguely remember someone coming to my door. I recall trying to talk to them. I remember the startled look on their face, like, "Oh my God! This pastor is wasted. He is blown out of his mind." And I was. I remember them slowly backing off the porch.

The reason I've mentioned this is because the Bible talks about being under the influence of the Holy Spirit. In Ephesians 5 the Word goes on to say, "... *don't be drunk with wine.*" If Paul were writing today, he might say, "*Don't be buzzed on the drugs.*" The amplified Bible says, "*Be filled and stimulated by the Holy Spirit.*" And the way you do that is through worship, singing hymns or spiritual songs, praying and giving thanks to God. When you receive the Word, the Holy Spirit fills you up. There is stimulation. A buzz happens. Have you ever experienced that? You came to church, the music was great, God's spirit was in the house, the Word was preached, and you walked out of that service different. You overcame some things. You were victorious. You entered the sanctuary worried about your marriage, your children, your finances or your relationship. Then you left church and you were buzzed. I say this because you and I can be under the influence of the Holy Spirit and really work through the painful issues of family blending.

There are some conflicts in a blended family that are never resolved. Laura and I have some conflicts we've never resolved. We just kept going another day and another day. The issues never went away. But at least we didn't go away. We could've quit. We could've walked away from one another. The issues were intense. The enemy of our souls would have loved to use it against us. I want to tell you that I understand that blending a family is tough stuff.

One of the reasons we are still together today and the reason we still have the deep intimate love that we have is because of a Biblical principle concerning anger and going to bed angry. Believe me, we've had some intense moments of fellowship. We've had some difficulty. But at the end of the day, we've made up. If we went to bed angry, we would not go to sleep angry. We would lay there for ten minutes, and then one of us would start a conversation, something like this:

"Well, are you going to pray or am I going to pray?"

"No, I'm not praying, you're going to have pray. I need another half hour before I'm fit to pray."
"Well, who's going to talk first?"
"Well, maybe the next time, it'll be me, but it isn't going to be me this time."

But at the end of the night, we always prayed. It might be two, three or four in the morning, but we always prayed. We got it done. That was in our early years. We don't have that difficulty now, but those early years were tough. The reason we are together today is because our Biblical foundation reminds us to do what God would require of us. Pray. We deliberately and intentionally put ourselves under the influence of the Holy Spirit.

Putting ourselves under the Holy Spirit's influence wasn't easy. At times our flesh and our wills were pulling against one another. My desires and hers were having a tug-of-war. I couldn't see what she was seeing and she couldn't see my perspective. At the end of the day, we had to put ourselves under the influence.

These loves we have mentioned, are the foundation for this book. Everything I'm going to tell you in this book is based on them. If you're not under the influence of the Holy Spirit and His love, you'll have a hard time with where to go from here.

Love is all about forgiveness. Christ voluntarily died on the cross for us. Do you think He wanted to do that? No, He really didn't want to, but He was so committed to this 'new covenant' – there's that word again 'covenant' – marriage, relationship, connection, covenant. He was so committed to it that He said:
Luke 22:42 *"Father, if you are willing, take this cup from me, yet not my will, but yours be done."*
Jesus was saying, *"Father if there is another way to get this job done, let's do it because I really don't want to go down this road. This is way too tough. But, if you ask me to, I will die to myself and my own wants and I will do it."*

Let's talk some more about covenant. This is very important. In the Old Testament, they practiced animal sacrifice. Animals died, symbolizing the importance of the covenant. Someone took a knife and cut the animal in two halves – right down the middle. One half of the calf would be laid out to the right of the person and the other half of the calf would be laid out to the left of the person. It was a bloody mess. The people that were coming into covenant with one another would walk into the middle of this bloody mess.

Basically what they were saying was this, "*An animal's life was given on behalf of this covenant we are entering into.*" Walking through these two halves was called, "*The Walk of Death.*" (I've had a personal practice of saying to a bride and groom standing before me in their wedding ceremony, "*You all are getting murdered, married, murdered, married.*" (Of course I'm joking around with them.) But in reality, it's the same thing. Marriage is death to self. Because they are coming together saying, "*Not my will be done, but yours – I'm deferring to you. I'm dying to myself.*" This act and this day was so important in the Old Testament day that the two entering into covenant were saying, "*If I break this covenant, then may the same thing that was done to this animal, be done to me.*" That's wild. That's Old Testament type covenant. That's how serious God took covenant. If you are starting a blended family because of a previous divorce, I am not judging you or condemning you for breaking a covenant. I'm just trying to help you to keep it from happening *again*. God has already forgiven you for anything that you have asked him to.

In the Garden of Eden, when Adam and Eve sinned, God's love was so intense for them that, even in their sin, God had a plan to send Christ to redeem them – all because of covenant love. That's incredible.

I call Ephesians 4:32 the KFC verse – the Kentucky Fried Chicken verse. Look at it:

*"And be **kind** one to another, tenderhearted, forgiving one another, even as God for **Christ's** sake hath forgiven you."*
Now you see how I remember scriptures. I attach them to food or something else familiar.
Be kind, be tenderhearted, and forgive one another. From time to time, in marriage and in blended families, we will experience all kinds of stretching, offenses, hurt and strife. We need to remember to be under the influence – be kind, tenderhearted and forgive one another. Try your best not to be abrasive. Avoid being hurtful at all costs.

Offenses just come. We can get offended by just about anything. Guys, has your wife ever asked you, *"What did you mean by that?"* Ladies, let me help you; he didn't mean anything by that. He didn't. Sometimes the wife will say, *"What are you thinking?"* Ladies, if he says, *"I'm not thinking anything."* Believe me, he's not thinking anything. Men don't think. If we look like we are zoned out, we probably are. There's nothing going on.

If we don't forgive, we are stuck in deep weeds. Think of the cross. The vertical member of the cross represents Christ's relationship with us. The horizontal member represents our relationship with one another. Do you know that horizontal member can be a hindrance to our prayers being answered? That horizontal member can block our relationship with God if we are not right with each other.
Colossians 3:13 NLT *"... you must make allowance for each other's faults and forgive the person who offends you. Remember, the Lord forgave you, so you must forgive others."*

Sometimes we don't want to hear this. But it's basic Bible foundations. If you don't get this, then when we get to ex-wives, ex- husbands – children and step children – moms, dads and step moms and dads we miss the whole point, and we set ourselves up for failure. Unless you lay the forgiveness building block in your relational foundation, your structure won't stand. We have got to make a decision before the offense or grievance comes. We've got to decide we are going to forgive ahead of time – before the offense happens. You know what really makes it cool? When the person you're married to knows you're going to forgive him/her before they get there. That's when love gets real reaches a new level. Because there is nothing like the safety and security that comes from, being unconditionally loved.

We didn't have that kind of strength early in our relationship. But now I can tell my wife anything. At this point in our journey we can look at each other and say, *"If you mess up, you're forgiven. I'm not going to hold anything against you."* We might get aggravated or irritated about something, but we know we're forgiven. At the end of day we will go on. We will not hold offense toward one another.

Remember the story Jesus told about the guy who borrowed a million dollars from the King? He went to the King and begged for forgiveness because he couldn't pay it back. Then the King decides to show him mercy and forgive him. Then the guy, just forgiven, goes to a guy who owed him seventeen dollars. When the guy didn't pay him, he had him locked up and thrown in prison. Remember that? When the King heard about it, he said, *"Turn that man over to the torturers."* Jesus says in Matthew 18 that that's how it will be for those who won't forgive.

"The human being who lives only for himself finally reaps nothing but unhappiness. Selfishness corrodes. Unselfishness ennobles, satisfies. Don't put off the joy derivable from doing helpful, kindly things for others." –BC Forbes

Love is about unselfishness. Love is about being selfless. Because of our culture and our parenting styles today, we have raised a group of people who are self-centered. It's all about me, me, and me. There's a philosophy today in marriage which says – God wants me happy at all costs. Even if we don't go so far as to say that, many act on that belief. I hear people say, "*Hey, God cares about my happiness.*"

Of course God wants us happy, but it's not the highest thing on His priority list. Many other things have priority over your happiness. Marriage is not about your happiness. I've never seen that in the Bible. God never says, "*I bring this man and this woman together in Holy Matrimony for their happiness.*" When we think our marriage is for the purpose of happiness, then we are on the brink of making a bad mistake.

I hope you are happy in your marriage. I will talk about the pathway to happiness in your marriage in the upcoming chapters. But you have to get these other areas in order first. Happiness won't come until you have selflessly and un-selfishly loved the other person. Prefer the other person. Serve the other person. Do for them. Wait on them.

When you say marriage is all about my happiness, you're actually saying, "*I'm an ego maniac – life is all about me.*" We can't be self-contained but we can conquer ourselves with God's help.
Ephesians 5:21 NLT *And further, you will submit to one another out of reverence for Christ.*

He is saying, "*Based on your relationship with Christ, being under the influence of that relationship, submit one to the other.*" Husbands, submit yourselves to your wives. Wives, submit yourselves to your husbands. Prefer, honor, and respect each other. The goal of a healthy marriage is not happiness. The goal is to reflect the image of Christ. Picture each other saying, "*Not my will be done Lord, but yours, but hers, but his.*" The Bible calls this a mystery and is talking about Christ and church. Think about this. Where else will people who are outside of the covenant see true covenant? Where will they see Jesus? One place they will see Jesus is in your marriage, your relationships, your family, and the way you relate to people. We are the body and we need to reach out and live our lives by example, or the world will shape us to its standards, instead of the standard of God's word. People will see Jesus when they see how a step-mother loves her step-children – unconditionally loving them, forgiving them, and treating them as if they were her own children. Those looking in from outside the home will see Jesus in the house, at the table, IN the marriage.

So the foundation is to be under the influence of God's unconditional love and favor at all times.

CHAPTER 2
TWO's A Crowd

How Do I Handle the Negativity?

Family blending is easier for adults than it is for children because we choose the change. Our children do not. Their lives are in our hands. Before making that choice for them, be sure that you have prayed about it, discussed it with them, and are confident that this is a lifetime decision. There are many factors that tug on the heart of a child when Mom or Dad marries someone else. Kids can't tell you all the different ways they hurt. Little ones may act out. Older children may tuck their head inside and hide their feelings. They are the victims of broken families. Most children feel cheated out of a normal life. In this section, along with my wife, I want to give you some counsel from God's word and from our own experience. We hope this will help you and your family.

Blended families have many different factors that contribute to the logic of how to handle things properly. Everyone has a unique idea of how things should be done. That is what makes navigating these waters difficult, risky, and downright dangerous.

Some of the hardest gaps to bridge are those between exes and new spouses. Sometimes an ex is bitter, immature, jealous, or unreasonable. Sometimes you are the one with those feelings. If that is true, then you need to let go of that anger before you even think about moving on. Blending a family while you still hold anger and resentment in your heart is a ticking time bomb. You will explode eventually and probably take out those frustrations on the wrong person. Letting go is the first step in moving on.

There are so many unresolved issues that a person can dwell on. Dwelling on those issues can cause a lot of negative emotions. Often the new spouse becomes the object of that negativity, even though the bad feelings can be misplaced. But it can cause the new spouse to become impractical, one-sided, jealous, bitter, or self-seeking. It can lead to periods of game playing. Things can escalate quickly and create problems that make a child's head spin. Our goal for this series is to give you some foundational structure that will help you navigate through the rough rapids of family blending.

God has an agenda for marriage and in order for us to fulfill that agenda, we need to follow His set of standards. First, we must understand God's definition of marriage. In a God-first marriage, spouses love and support each other the way that God loves his church. Everyone works together for the common good. Our second priority is our relationship with God. We must develop a Christ consciousness that keeps Principle first in our lives. Learn to be able to get to God in 30 seconds or less at any time. This can help you keep your cool in difficult situations. Finally, renew your commitment to put your marriage before children and family. Marriage is second only to your relationship with God. This can be so hard sometimes because the love that we have for our children is so different than the love that we have for each other. Remember the types of love that we spoke about in the last chapter. As parents, we are like God with that Agape love for his children, as we have for our own. The love between a husband and wife is different, and sometimes that can cloud our view of different situations. It is often easier to unconditionally love a child that came from our own DNA, than it is to unconditionally love our spouse, who many times is so opposite of our self.

God directs us to take our children out of the number one role and put our marriages first. You heard it. Husbands, your loyalty goes to your wife before your biological child. Wives, your loyalty goes to your husband before your biological child. But you must be worthy of your spouse's loyalty. If you are trampling on it by acting immature, self-centered, irrational, or jealous, your spouse will have a hard time trusting you. God's assignment is not a game. Respect is the key factor in this arena. No matter how much your gut is screaming at you that your husband or wife is wrong in a situation that involves your children, you have to step back, get in to God, and remember that you have to respect your spouse's opinion on the situation.

Genesis 2:24 *For this reason a man will leave his father and mother and be united to his wife, and they will become one flesh.*

Work to keep the spark in your marriage. Invest in it. Date each other. If possible, plan to take a weekend away from the kids from time to time to keep your romance alive. Kids join our lives, we don't join theirs, and they grow up and leave. So stay intimately connected to each other.

Ephesians 6:1 *Children, obey your parents in the Lord, for this is right.*

Deuteronomy 6:5-9 *"And you shall love the Lord your God with all your heart and with all your soul and with all your might. [6] "And these words, which I am commanding you today, shall be on your heart; [7] and you shall teach them diligently to your sons and shall talk of them when you sit in your house and when you walk by the way and when you lie down and when you rise up. [8] "And you shall bind them as a sign on your hand and they shall be as frontals on your forehead. [9] "And you shall write them on the doorposts of your house and on your gates.*

Know Your Role

What is our role? What are our goals and our purpose for parenting? According to God's word, our role is to teach our children how to live a God-first life. There are many different learning styles. Some learn by listening, some by seeing, and some by doing. But our job is to set an example that teaches at all these levels.

Most of my scripting comes from the things that I learned by watching what my parents did. They didn't direct my attention to what they were doing, but I observed it all − even what they didn't want me to see. And many of the things I observed are the way I automatically do things today. So we must live our lives with deliberate intention. Our goal is to train our children so well that the ways of God are imprinted upon them. Our purpose is to prepare them to become independent and leave, spreading the message of hope. We must teach children to obey God's word, and lead by our example, showing the way. How do we that? By loving them, bringing them to church and reading stories. The Bible is rich with the stories explaining the sacred way. Reading children's Bible stories over and over until the child knows them by heart without reading a word, is a good way to teach. There are many. Get your children into the children's programs in your local church and let some of God's helpers inspire them as they blossom and bloom. Psalm 25:12 *Who is the man who reverently fears and worships the Lord? Him shall He teach in the way that he should choose.*

The reason that God hardwired us the way He did was for His agenda and for His purpose. But how can we find out what that is? I'm not sure we ever know EXACTLY, but God gives us clues. His agenda is so big that there are endless opportunities to serve. If an activity appeals to your child, then enroll him or her. God can work through any activity. There is no talent that is unacceptable to God. As with all clues, one thing leads to another, and before long the happiness of good work shines the Light of Christ through your children. Happiness and success help guide your child into his or her divine niche. It allows both of you to take a look at natural gifts, talents, and abilities. What are your child's strengths? When do things come most naturally? Where is he or she happiest? These answers can help you guide them into purpose. Be careful here. Don't try to bend your kids to fit your agenda. Many parents live vicariously through their children. Each one of us has a separate, sacred purpose. We are all gifted. We each have a purpose in His kingdom. We are all important to God. Help your children make a connection to God. Teach them to see their value and worth. Help them understand who they are in Christ. Show them how to give Him praise for their inheritance – their gifts.

Make Memories

Think back to your first memory of God. My faith is so deeply embedded in me that I can't remember a time when I didn't know about God. How did that happen? My parents were people of faith. How did they become believers? Their parents. Maybe you grew up in a home that didn't have God in it, and then you found Him later in life. You may have a history of alcoholism or infidelity in your family. In some cases, that makes you even more special. You get the opportunity to be the one who makes a change, the one who creates a greater destiny for your family and a name for them in heaven. Leadership is, simply put, making the destination and the way clear. God's kingdom is the destination, and living a life that honors His Church is the way. That's not so hard, is it? The way is easy for us because He sent his only begotten son to die on the cross for our sins. All we have to do is WANT salvation and we have it. When our kids see how happy and fulfilled we are in Christ, their wanting will occur naturally.

Good Kids Gone Bad (for a moment)

Even good kids can make bad decisions. Temptation abounds. We can protect them when they're home, but eventually they begin to mix with people from all walks of life. This becomes the time when they get to practice the skills we referred to previously – forging relationships that challenge us, grow us, and shape our direction. Discovering how they fit with peers can cause them to test limits and cross lines. We need to know how to handle that when it happens. It will happen. Discipline can take many forms.

Hebrews 12:11 *No discipline is enjoyable while it is happening—it is painful! But afterward there will be a quiet harvest of right living for those who are trained in this way.* We are all familiar with time out techniques and spanking. This subject continues to be a politically heated debate. There is controversy about the effectiveness of punishment on children. My question is whether or not we get to pick and choose what the Bible teaches. The Bible presents clear guidance. We agree that it provides the foundation for living a proper life. So how do we reconcile the concept of spanking?

Perhaps our answer is farther back than the point at which we feel we have to spank a child. Is it possible to look with better eyes and examine what fuels our belief that our only recourse is to strike out at a person we love? Could we find a better way? Perhaps as parents we only use it because we get to the end of our ropes. Sometimes we haven't set up boundaries or clear limits for our children. When there aren't limits, kids push parents as far as they can.

There's an old saying, 'Spare the rod, spoil the child.' This passage about the rod invokes fear. But on the other hand, 'Thy rod and Thy staff shall comfort me.' This passage invokes peace. Perhaps there are two ways to view the staff. Early in life I feared the wrath of a punishing God, and saw the staff as an instrument for beating someone into submission. But now, through the eyes of a loving God, or when I look with agape love, I see the staff as an extension to help lift another, to help them up. It is a crutch, a chance to let God help hold us up in times of trouble. So many things in life are all about perspective. There isn't a moment in your lifetime that you are done learning. When it comes to our children, we have to learn to look at things from a perspective that is not our own. It is the only way that we can even come close to seeing "both sides of the story." Perhaps we need only look differently in order to gain a completely different perspective. In Ingram's book, *Passionate Presence*, there is a story that reminds us about perspective.

A few years ago I was with a close friend in a grocery store. As we snaked along the aisles, we became aware of a mother with a small boy going in the opposite direction and passing us in each aisle. The woman barely noticed us because she was so furious with her child, who seemed intent on pulling items off the lower shelves. As the mother became more and more frustrated, she started to yell at her son and several aisles later, progressed to shaking him by the arm.

At this point my friend spoke up. A wonderful mother of three and founder of a progressive school, she had probably never in her life treated any child so harshly. I expected that my friend would give this woman a solid mother-to-mother talk about controlling herself and about the effect this kind of behavior has on a child. Braced for a confrontation, I felt a spike of adrenaline.

Instead my friend said, "What a beautiful little boy. How old is he?" The woman answered cautiously, "He's 3." My friend went on to say how curious he seemed and how her own three children behaved in the grocery store, pulling things off shelves, so interested in all the wonderful colors and packages. "He seems so bright and intelligent," my friend said. The woman had the boy in her arms by now and a shy smile came to her face. Gently brushing the hair out of his eyes, she said, "Yes, he's very smart and curious, but sometimes he wears me out." My friend responded sympathetically, "They can do that; they're so full of energy."

As we walked away, I heard the mother speaking more kindly to the boy about getting home and cooking his dinner. "We'll have your favorite—macaroni and cheese," she told him.

If you don't need to prove that you are right or that someone else's behavior should be punished, you can better see your way to achieving harmony in any given situation. My friend instinctively knew that reprimanding the mother in the grocery store might have incited her to greater rage—rage that might later have been directed at the child. Although there are times when it is necessary to stop someone from physically hurting another person, more often it is helpful that we show love and understanding to those lost in anger, allowing them to remember their own tenderness.

Each of us can share tender mercies throughout the day. These small kindnesses toward friends, family or strangers may go unnoticed by the world at large, but in offering them, by letting love flow through us, we will generate a field of sacredness. And that is its own reward.

The love that you show to others when no one is watching; the love that no one will praise you for, is the purest love that you will ever express to another.

In this excerpt, the mother is extremely frustrated by what she interprets as the actions of a disobedient child. She thinks she wants a quiet child who just sits still in the cart. In her frustration, she can't see from the child's perspective. She doesn't know how to get what she wants. When we ask God for help, he sends a person. So along comes an observant stranger to help her see differently. With a different focus, she sees that she actually DOES have what she wants, a brilliant, curious, healthy, active child.

Proverbs 22:15 *Foolishness is bound up in the heart of a child; The rod of discipline will remove it far from him.*

Nowhere in this passage does it say that foolishness is bad. It just refers to the heart of a child. WE shape what a child deems good or bad behavior by the meaning we attach to things. So it is up to US to either thrust the rod or extend it. We will act through our own interpretation. In the excerpt, the frustrated mom acts out of her best understanding of the situation and interprets appropriate discipline (the rod) as a violent shaking. The other shopper interprets the appropriate action (the rod) as a tool to create clarity about the child's intention. Can you see the choice? Sometimes we just need to step back and ask for clarity. Ask and you shall receive.

I think that's why it's so important to be on the same page as parents. We must unify and create a strong position with agreed upon limits and set consequences for crossing the line. We must rest our frustration and desperation in God's hands and enter into His perfect solution. We must chisel away at the conditions that have brought us to this point of misalignment and begin to reshape our relationships. God can turn us from batterers to *betterers*. Sometimes it just one thought, one impulse well controlled, or one prayer away. But one thing never changes – God's love. He loves us because of who He is, not because of anything we do or don't do. Relationships take practice. Nobody is perfect. We make mistakes, just like our kids. They need us to guide, instruct, teach, correct, and rebuke. They also need forgiveness, just like us. They need to know that God and their parents have their backs. And that's the truth.

Proverbs 13:24 *He who spares the rod hates his son, but he who loves him is careful to discipline him.*

Do's and Don'ts of Discipline

Laura and I want to share some things we've learned raising our family. First Laura will share some ideas and then I will. The purpose of presenting both is to help illustrate how much richer joint parenting is. Handling everything ourselves limits us to what we know. I've always believed the saying that two heads are better than one.

Do's

1) Agree with your ex as much as possible on affirmative plans that focus on the needs of the children, but also protect your newly formed family. It's easier to keep agreements and plans when they benefit everyone. Showing unconditional love for everyone, even someone that may have mistreated you, is something that your children will watch intently.

2) Agree not to bad mouth, or allow your children to bad mouth, your ex or step. One way to practice that is to keep the conversation on point. Take the focus off the person and put it back on the subject you need to discuss. If it's behavior, focus on the action or lack of action that is unacceptable and why. Leave the person out of it. Teach kids tolerance for the differences of others. Ultimately, it offers them added richness by providing more than one way of getting to the same end. Creative expression is joyful. If you can't agree with the way you do things at your house or your ex does things there, perhaps you can all find a new way to do things.

3) Agree on boundaries and behavioral guidelines as much as possible. It's important to remember that when you had your kids you agreed upon a set of guidelines by which to raise them. Unless something has happened to drastically change the way you feel about raising them, why not

present a strong, united front. Both of you still want to raise great kids.

4) Understand that children are prone to test the boundaries, manipulate, especially if they can play one spouse against the other to gain something. Formal learning teaches us to understand rules and boundaries, question other people's conclusions, and to be inventive. As adults, it's important to remember how many ways there are to do that. We just have to refocus behavior that varies from acceptable norms and get it turned around. Again, focus on the actions, not the person.

5) If possible compare notes. Although it may be painful, keep each other informed. You are both after the same end result. Consistency creates a nurturing environment for children to learn and explore ideas. It provides them a safe place to process what's happening outside of home in the context of the core beliefs they share with you at home. Make it easy for them. A God-first life honors everyone, both inside and outside the home.

6) Commit to conduct yourself with emotional integrity. Don't try to twist things to suit your position. Create a safe space for everyone to say how they truly feel. Most of our problems stem from some basic misunderstanding or lack of information.

7) Make your house a house of peace. Make 'home' the place everybody wants to be.

8) Make your own unique traditions. They don't have to be fancy, just fun. Whether it's tying balloons to the birthday person's toes or having breakfast for supper, enjoy each other! Example: Bedtime at our house is a routine. We rotate which child's room we pray in. We all go to that room, and every child must pray for one thing and then thank God for one thing that made their lives happy that day.

9) Be quick to repent. If you mess up, own it. Apologize. Tell each other how much you care and that you will try hard not to repeat your mistake. Make it right. Then turn away from it, and get back on the path of Love.

10) Be quick to forgive. 'Forgive us our trespasses as we forgive those who trespass against us.' After you've accepted or rendered an apology, forgive yourself. We have a tendency to hold onto things that don't serve us well. Receive the forgiveness and grace you extend to others.

11) Teach your children to dream. We all feel better when we have something to look forward to. Teach planning so that they can measure their progress. Charting progress helps inspire them to continue on. Begin to practice using faith early. Faith builds character. Working toward and achieving dreams builds confidence and breeds success in all areas of life. We want our kids to know that they can aspire to anything God calls them to do, and do it well.

12) When things just aren't working out naturally, take responsibility. Don't waste time blaming. Take the high road. Find a better way. Most of the great inventors can tell you that they failed many times on the way to their greatest work. Give yourself that freedom. God does. Show your kids that you can work things out and find good solutions together. Through God all things are possible.

Don'ts

1) Don't speak out in anger. Control your temper with spouses and children. Once you say something, you can't take it back.

2) Don't treat children as small adults. They should not be your buddies because you are emotionally hurting. Do NOT confide in your children. Call a friend or close family member for that.

3) Don't depend too much on young children for companionship and support because you are hurt. I've known lonely parents who wrap their whole identity up in their kids in an attempt to fill the void. This cheats you both.

4) Don't use bribery, use motivation. Teach them what is right. Inspire them to love well. Goodness fills you up and starts a chain reaction of good that can light up a family. Enable everyone to shine.

5) Don't be wishy-washy. Inconsistent discipline creates confusion. Agree on rules and don't be afraid to hold a child's feet to the line.

6) Don't punish – discipline. Children know when they've done something wrong. Honoring boundaries and keeping agreements contributes to a healthy self-esteem, and helps create confidence.

7) Don't sabotage your child's relationship with your ex. The way to get respect is to give it. No matter how small your child is, like I said before, they are always watching. As they grow, they will see who acted appropriately and who did not. Live an honorable life and uphold an honorable relationship, and your child will honor you.

8) Don't use your child as a pawn to get even or manipulate, or control, or even threaten your ex. They're not ping pong balls, they're our precious children. Their feelings are fragile. If a home cannot be a place of refuge and peace, where will they go? What might they turn to for feeling good?

9) Don't use your children to gain information. If you want to know something about your ex, ask them. 'Ask and you shall receive.'

10) Don't transfer feelings upon your children. This can be hard when they look like your ex and even harder if they exhibit a behavior that mimics your ex. Example: "You are acting just like your FATHER." Don't do it. Getting those few words out are not worth the years of remembrance that your child will have of you saying them.

11) Don't force your child to choose sides in conflict in your own home or at your ex's. Children need protection from adult issues. They have many other changes to integrate into their lives as a result of all the adjustments they've been forced to make. Trust your children to continue to love you as much as ever. Trust God to keep their hearts open. Trust God. I can't emphasize those two words enough. YOU have to have faith or you will go crazy.

12) Don't be emotionally needy with your children. Kids have their own issues to cope with. If you're suffering, talk to the prayer ministers or your pastor. Call a friend or loved one,

but don't overburden your children by becoming overly needy.

13) Don't convert your own guilt into overindulgence of your children. Things don't equate to love. I've known many children who equate time spent with them as love. Know that children want to love you and want you to love them no matter what. Appease your guilt by offering them the peace and comfort of Christ. Play, work, and pray together. You can't buy love or peace.

Deuteronomy 6:5-9 *"And you shall love the Lord your God with all your heart and with all your soul and with all your might. [6] "And these words, which I am commanding you today, shall be on your heart; [7] and you shall teach them diligently to your sons and shall talk of them when you sit in your house and when you walk by the way and when you lie down and when you rise up. [8] "And you shall bind them as a sign on your hand and they shall be as frontals on your forehead. [9] "And you shall write them on the doorposts of your house and on your gates.*

While the kids are still at home, we are teachers, trainers, disciplinarians, and providers. It is a very hands on job. Our skills and abilities adapt and change. We want to be attentive to the cultivation of a rich spiritual life. This helps us all adapt to growth and changes. We all know that change is the only constant. And before we know it, they will grow up and leave home. (hopefully!) Then we will be friends, advisors, and counselors. Sometimes we are even the students. What we can give our kids that matters most is our Love and the gift of TIME.

What I've Learned

What kids need most from a father are time and touch. Recent studies report that our children need 100 touches a day. From the moment we are born, we need touch. It helps us bond to our family. It helps us feel attached. Holding a child makes them feel safe, loved, and comforted. This can be very grounding and bring peace to our children. As dads, don't be afraid to hug your boys, at least while they're young enough to let you.

Honest communication keeps us in touch with our kids. Talk to them at their level. Talk about what interests them. Tell them what interests you. Talk about things that may be uncomfortable for you. Force yourself to talk anyway. Keep the conversation balanced. It's important for kids to have a safe place to explore thoughts and feelings. We don't want them to learn important information or values from strangers. Even though some subjects will be hard for kids to approach, if you stay close and involved, you'll sense what might be just below the surface. And remember not to tell them more than they need to know.

Tenderness is both a masculine and feminine personality trait. Overdose your children on love. Show your soft underbelly. Every child deserves to have at least one person in their life that is crazy about them. Don't you love feeling favored? I remember once when my teacher told me I was her favorite. I tried harder than ever to be the ideal student. Some years later, at a class reunion, I found out that she told all her students the same thing. Perhaps her love was a lot like God's, who loves everyone with everything He has. Each and every one of us is favored. Living up to that love is what creates a God-first life.

Teach. You have an opportunity to teach every day. Do you recognize that opportunity? Sometimes things can be right in front of us and we can't see it. Have you ever been looking for your sunglasses and then you had them on the top of your head? Me, too. That's what I'm talking about. Don't let opportunity pass you by. Teach your kids to hope, believe, dream, and forgive. Give them the freedom of choice to go negative or to go positive.

They will exercise that choice if they know you are rock solid no matter what. Model the positive side.

Be tenacious. Never quit. Hold fast to your principles. It builds the value in. When something or someone is important to you, everyone knows it. Be sure to remind your children how special they are every day. Make sure that your children see how important that your spouse is to you as well. The more often your children laugh quiet giggles and say "gross" behind you after you give your husband or wife a kiss, the better. I don't know if I can say this enough: They are ALWAYS watching.

Recognize each child's uniqueness. Everyone is great in some ways. That's the beauty of remaining grounded. When kids don't have to worry about adult issues, they can immerse themselves in their creative bliss and discover just how unique and precious they are. Reinforce their creativity and uniqueness. Put their coloring on the refrigerator. Display their artwork proudly. Encourage them to develop further by enrolling them in a sport, class, drama club, chorus, or other organization that can help them grow their gifts. You could even take time to join them in their pursuits, showing them the most precious proof of love you have – your time. You only get one chance to do this, to be a parent. Don't let your amazing gifts grow up and be left with regret.

Utilize every single second of the day as an opportunity to teach, love and admire your children.

Embrace the ultimate goal of parenting – working yourself out of a job! Teach your children to become independent. Teach them the value of a God-first life. Show them that in all the changes and challenges of life, they are competent to find solutions. Let them work through difficult situations on their own. Stay close, but don't interfere unless it's absolutely necessary. Nothing sends a stronger message to a child that he or she is not capable faster than doing things for them. And remember that your way may not be the only way. Trust God and your child. Let every situation bring out the best in you both.

Sibling Rivalry

When the step children don't get along, what can you do?

First and foremost, be in unity. Keep your marriage first. This can be difficult at times. Children want to believe that they are the most important people in your life. Children may feel that there are sides: Mom or Dad's side with them, and Step-Mom or Step-Dad's side against them. You can assure them that they are very important to you and so is your spouse. Show them that the Bible leads us in ways that have the best interest of everyone in mind. Take yourself out of the driver's seat and put God in charge. Sometimes just knowing that God, not the parent or step-parent in question, is setting the direction can diffuse the situation.

Let your children know that they can confide in you. Let them know that if they do have a problem you will not discuss it in front of the other children. There are times that siblings will be at odds. First, talk to each one separately. If you need to, bring them together afterwards and let them work amicably through to a mutually agreed upon solution. Then let that be the end of it. Keep it private. The only thing worse than making a mistake is having it made public. Shame is a powerful emotion. It can undermine a child's self-esteem. Let your children know that their feelings move only from their lips to your heart and into God's ear; that they are safe.

If the mistake is grave, then you will have to enter into an honest dialogue with the child about the consequences of their actions. Do not feel sorry for them. It can be a mistake. Teach them about cause and effect. There are consequences for every action. If you put good things in, good comes out, and vice versa. But keep the focus on the action. The child is not bad, but the choice is unacceptable.

Be truthful. Kids are smart. If you try to deceive them or say something halfheartedly, they'll detect it. They may not be able to name it, but they won't recognize it as the truth. They'll sense that things are not what they seem. This chips away at your credibility and teaches them that in some circumstances it's okay to be dishonest.

Teach them that things aren't always fair. Children seem to know intuitively when things are not fair. It can happen anywhere. Things happen at school or at a sporting event. When judgment errors are made, they are final. We can't change them. Frequently, kids use fairness as a fall-back argument to try to get their way. When they work through their bag of tricks and find no power in them, then they pull out 'that's not fair.' Then the bargaining begins. It's better to get some power than none. This is the time to really reinforce the power in unity. Instead of compromising your parenting position, thereby creating a solution that's only halfway acceptable to you both, work together to find a solution that makes you both winners. It's there if you look. It's so empowering to teach a child how to work through a problem to the answer that declares everyone a winner.

Confront *jealousy* for what it is. Most people patty-cake all around identifying jealousy for what it is. Jealousy stems from a feeling of lack. Its roots are in a belief that there's not enough to go around, whether it is love, money, food, attention, time, or anything else. Dispel jealousy with love. Talk to your child and find out what's really behind the behavior you're observing. Explain that lack is simply a perception. As soon as you take the power out of the belief in lack, the behavior will stop. Reassure the child that just because new people become important doesn't mean that the old ones are less important. It means that we add more love to the family. Celebrate ALL the members of your family. You can't make it happen, but you sure can model it.

Teach them to identify the good in their step family. Continue to point out all the things they have in common. Remind them that their step family is experiencing the same losses and victories that they are. Let them know that they can talk to you any time about things that make them uncomfortable, but encourage them to go direct to the source of a disagreement. Coach them about expressing their unhappiness without blaming. Teach them to trust their new family member enough to let them know when they've been offended or had their feelings hurt. Sometimes we misinterpret things. We always fill in the blanks from our own experience. Rather than lingering in a bad place, ask for clarity. Then work from there.

Joke with them. A sense of humor goes a long, long way. Laughter is very therapeutic. Mother Nature hardwired us to laugh. It helps us heal our bodies and emotions. It's a coping mechanism that helps us manage stress.
Blending is stressful, but worth it. Laughter is a medicine that feels and tastes really good. And it's FREE!

Spend time with children individually. Develop special relationships with each person. There is so much to gain from one another. Learn what each child is good at, passionate about, failing in, and thankful for. Relating at the level of soul, talking about what's REALLY on the child's mind is paramount to developing lasting closeness. Don't just scratch the surface, dig deep. It can be hard if your child is talented in an area that you aren't familiar with. If you have a son that loves to dance, it may be hard for a father to identify with this idea without a whole plethora of feelings overwhelming them. Remember what I said earlier about your children's gifts. God gave that gift to your child for a reason. Let them embrace it and have FAITH that your strong, all-knowing God has a plan.

Faith Spells Success

Set your children up for success. Don't waste precious time looking at what you DON'T want. Focus all your time and energy looking at what you do want. The way to extinguish bad behavior is to remove attention from it. Encourage success by rewarding it with attention. Live in success with your child. Praise, plan, pray and commit resources to your child's vision. This will give you both real powers. You will attract with those thoughts. Talk about the dreams that your children have for that success; help them decide what they may want to be or do with their lives; lead them to ideas that support their talents, but let them choose the path.

Did you know that there is never one pre-determined type or sex of sheep that leads the flock? It's not the eldest male or the wisest female. Research has shown that it is simply the one sheep that has decided to move. Initiative. That one sheep moves and the flock follows. Move. Give your children the initiative, and they will follow the Shepherd.

The kids will grow up soon. Love each other while they are growing up, and your family will blossom and bloom.

CHAPTER 3
THREE Sides to Every Story

Can You Help Me Choose the Right Priority?

"I don't care Troy. I'm just sick and tired of having this conversation over and over again."

"We've never finished this conversation, Suzanne. We always knock heads about this, but we never come to a resolution."

"What, you think we're going to resolve it now?"

"Well, obviously not now. I'm just saying we need to be in agreement on this – and we never have been."

"Well, I don't see how we can be in agreement when your step- mom bulldozes her way into our lives every time we see her."

"Well, she's just trying to be helpful."

"Helpful! I know she liked your ex-wife better than me, and she's never let me forget about it."

"No, that's not it."

"Oh really? What is it then?"

"She thinks that you don't give Jonathon the credit he deserves."

"Like what?"

"Like when he takes out the trash – cleans his room and does all of his chores without being asked."

"He's your son – shouldn't he get that support from you?"

"It would help if he got support from both of us. "I treat Sarah as if she were my own daughter."

"I know and I don't like the way you discipline her."

"What?"

"You grounded her for no reason, Troy."

"I don't call spilling Kool-Aid all over my research paper *no* reason."

"It was an accident and you would have never grounded Jonathan for something like that and you know it."

"I have had to ground Jonathan for doing that before – thank you very much – and for other things even less important."

"All I'm saying is, 'I have to hear about it every time I pick up her up from her dad. She's constantly complaining about how much harder you are on her than her own father is."

"Well, I can see why – he's the party dad. When was the last time he's had Sarah for more than a weekend? Didn't your custody agreement say he'd have her for a few weeks at a time during the year?"

"You know he can't have her during the school year. It's too far from the school and he doesn't have time to drive her."

"And yet conveniently, he finds himself out of town on business almost all summer long."

"Oh, you're one to talk about business. How about all the hours you spend down at the plant?"

"I wouldn't have to put all those hours in at the plant if my ex-wife would just marry that man she's living with. Until then, we are still shelling out alimony payments."

"Oh, I get it. You work for your ex-wife, but you don't have time to spend with your wife."

"Oh, come on!"

"I'm serious, Troy. We hardly have time to be husband and wife anymore. We are never alone together. We are always busy with work or the kids' school or keeping them from fighting one another."

"Can I help it if I want us to live in a happy home?"

"You call this happy? We argue all the time?"

"I know."

"I want a husband who wants to be with me, Troy. That's why I got divorced in the first place."

"I do want to be with you."

"Then come home after work."

"Do not make this about your estranged father, ok! I'm not him."

"Then stop acting like him."

"Your father left. I didn't. Do not put me on the same page as him."

"All right. Okay. We have to get out there on stage, the people are waiting."

"Are we going to talk about this?"

"Yes, Troy! Fine. Later. Let's just get out there and get this performance over with so we can get home and not spend any time together."
"Well, that sounds just fine to me."
"Good!"
"Fine!"

Unfortunately, this scene has played out in real life dramas more than we know.

One thing I've learned through twenty four years of married life and living in a blended family is this, 'Happy wife, happy life." You married couples already know that. If you're not married yet, write it down – and not on tissue paper either. Get a stone tablet and a chisel. It's commandment number eleven if you're counting.

Florence Henderson as Cinderella's Evil Stepmother:

Laura's Take
Pastor Daren, my husband, has already told you his story of his first marriage and his divorce in chapter 1. I want to give you a little bit of my perspective. I never really knew divorce. I grew up in a home where my parents stayed together. My mom went home to be with the Lord six months before we got married. That was very painful for me. My grandparents on both sides of the family stayed married. My dad's side of the family stayed together. All of his aunts and uncles remained married. There is very little, if any, divorce in my family history. The only thing I really knew about divorce and step parents is from what I saw as a child. Remember Cinderella? That was a terrifying thing for me. I remember that horrible step-mother and those ugly step-sisters. Remember how mean and evil they were? So that was my frame of reference.

Then the Brady Bunch came along. They were on the other end of the spectrum. Frankly, that was a little scary to me also. So you have two extremes here, and that was the only frame of reference I knew. So preparing for married life, for me, was a little bit shaky.

I really believe in preparation. I'm a person that plans and prepares. I believe God likes us to plan ahead of time. So before Daren and I got married, I really had to wrap my mind around, 'What does it really mean to be a step mother?' I know God hates divorce and that it's not His perfect will, but we are living in a fallen world. People are human and divorce happens. Blended families come together. Blended families don't always come together because of divorce. Sometimes it's a death, an adoption, or a racially mixed family. Blended families come about in all forms.

Daren: When you have a blended family, you simply have to set some priorities. Priorities are huge. The first priority for you is your personal relationship with God. Then your family's relationship with God is huge. But right under your relationship with God is your marriage. This is the hardest thing for blended families because the tendency, especially in our culture, is to put kids first. Even non-blended families lean toward this. Our culture promotes a 'kids first' mind set. Wrong. It's marriage first, then kids. It actually brings security to your children. After marriage, the next priority is still not the kids; it's the family as a family unit. Then the next priority is the individual children.

Good examples of blended families are found throughout the Bible. Moses was part of a blended family. Moses married an Ethiopian woman, which caused considerable controversy. Moses' marriage was the first recorded interracial marriage. Look at King David's life. He had several children from different wives. Even Jesus Himself was part of a blended family to a degree, because He was raised by His step-father, Joseph. His real father was Father God. So Jesus can relate to blended family issues.

Laura: In preparing for my blended family experience and preparing to be a step mother, I went to the Word. The Bible helped me wrap my mind around the role of being a step mom. I said, "Ok, God, you hate divorce. I'm going to stay married to this man. I'm going to stay committed to him one hundred percent. I'm not going back on that commitment. Here's the thing, when I looked at his children, I refused to have unrealistic expectations. So many times we can get ourselves into trouble with our expectations. You know, I fell in love with Daren, but I didn't necessarily fall in love with the children right away. That process happened over time.

Children are not necessarily going to fall in love with step-parents right away either. You see, they are still in a grieving process. The death of a parent or a divorce is the loss of security, a loss of life as they know it. It's a very painful thing, especially for the children. Healing doesn't take place for them as expeditiously as it might for adults. The kids are still hurting. Pain is most likely still there. I had to make a decision.

I made a decision to love those children as if they were my own – despite bad behavior. This was my commitment. None of us know the unexpected. Can you ever totally prepare for marriage? No. But getting some good Bible principles under your belt before you enter a marriage can truly help. Are you ever prepared for being a step-parent? No. There are always unexpected things in life. It's the commitments you make in your life that will sustain you through those hard times. I never changed or wavered on my commitment to stay married to this man and to love his children unconditionally. And it was not always easy.

Daren: One of the first things we had to deal with when we were married was establishing boundaries. We had to set boundaries. I would encourage you to set some boundaries. Boundaries will keep your relationship healthy. Henry Cloud and John Townsend wrote an excellent book on this subject. It is called *Boundaries: When to Say Yes, How to Say No to Take Control of Your Life.* If you're struggling with in-laws or children you'll love this book.

In our relationship, we had joint custody of our two girls. The girls lived with their mother, and they would be with us every other weekend. So that meant we would pick them up on a Friday and take them back on a Sunday afternoon. So we actually had them for a total of forty-eight hours every two weeks. They would be with us only four days out of the month. That was hard. What happened during those four days was challenging. The girls would come over with a 'to-do list' for *us* from their mother. A to-do list for the whole weekend!

"Here's a list. My mom said you need to take us to the Magic House, take us to the Zoo, and you need to take us here and there." So we had to set boundaries and say, "We are not doing what your momma wants us to do. We have our own plans."

Another important factor was our relatives who wanted to spend time with the girls. They could only get them on the weekends that we had them, so if they got them we didn't. We just had to set boundaries.

Laura: "Don't be too hard on your family – this is new to them, too. They are also trying to navigate these waters. You have grandparents, aunts and uncles, and they all love your children dearly. But what you have to do is set priorities.

What are the priorities of a child? The number one thing they need is to be with their parents. Unfortunately they have a broken home now. Their number one priority is to spend time with the parent they don't live with.

You see it's not just you and your children that go through a divorce. Everybody goes through a divorce. That's one reason God hates it so much. Children are affected, grandparents are affected, aunts and uncles are affected, friends and so on – everyone is affected. You have to do this in love. You have to be patient and kind. We set a priority for other relatives to get the girls when it was not our weekend to have them. We give you permission to call the ex-wife, the ex-husband. Make arrangements with them and make sure it's not on our weekend. We would never prevent them from seeing the girls, but we asked for them to respect our priorities.

Daren: Create a sense of security and peace in your home. The greatest gift you can give your family besides introducing them to Christ and raising them in a local church is the gift of a peaceful life, free of the worry that mom and dad might get divorced *again* someday.

Anybody can create a sense of security, whether you're in a blended family or not. The most valuable thing you can give your children is the security of a good marriage. We gave special attention to the things that would bring peace to our marriage because the children's world had been turned upside down. Think of traveling on an airline. The flight attendant is giving the safety talk just before take-off. "If there is a loss of cabin pressure, a yellow mask will drop from the overhead compartment. Put your mask on first – then put them on the children." If you put the mask on your child first, then by the time you do that you'll be passed out. You'll die. If you put the children ahead of your marriage, you'll pass out, the marriage can die. By taking care of yourself first, you can take better care of the children.

Laura: The number one thing you need to work on is how you resolve conflict. You can't hear this enough. You have to work at it. It is so easy to get caught up in the moment, to allow a flurry of emotions to run rampant. You can't afford to do that. You must not resolve conflicts or have all out wars in front of the children.

Do you realize what it does to the heart of a child when you argue or have heated discussions in front of them? Imagine how devastating it is when the issue being discussed is about them. And many of the issues in blended families are about them. It is so painful for the child.

One of the commitments we made in the beginning our marriage was to never talk badly about his ex-wife. We did not do that. If I would have been married before, he would have made the same commitment to me. You may have had issues and you may have been hurt. You may still be in pain and grieving. Children are just not able to handle the burden of adult issues. They are not wired to handle it. They can't be your confidante. You must not spill verbal venom into the child. Maybe you were the great parent and your ex was horrible, maybe even abusive. But those are issues for adults to pursue legally. Maybe they weren't a good husband or a good wife. Maybe they had adulterous affairs on you. Maybe they weren't there for you. Children need to be able to love their parents unconditionally. Whether your ex was a good husband of wife or not, your children need to feel free to love them without hearing you bad mouth their mom or dad. To tear down your ex in front of your child is very destructive.

Now that the girls are grown and fully matured, they have asked questions about the past. We speak the truth to them, and we do it in love. We answer them honestly. We tell them how it really worked and how it was. Sometimes we discovered they were told a lie. The truth needs to come out. When they are mature enough to handle some of the issues, then you tell them the truth, but not when they are children. Keep them protected.

Daren: Don't trash talk your ex to your children. Love is the foundation for a healthy family life. When your children are grown, things can be said, that will explain the truth. As long as you have stood steadfast as a parent, they will understand and be thankful that you let them make the decisions about their other parent.

A conflict riddled home makes for a lot of insecurity for the children. Try to eliminate the verbal put downs from your families altogether. Children's needs are easily categorized. Their first and primary need is security. Secondly, they need acceptance. Thirdly, they crave unconditional love and affirmation. And last but not least, they need boundaries. Boundaries help keep them in check. Your child will never tell you they want boundaries. But without boundaries they will have insecurity. Things get crazy without boundaries.

Laura: Another thing we work on is having fun. Life at home should be fun because life, away from home, can be so serious. We made a point to start new traditions. You've started a new family. You're building on broken dreams. Nobody gets married and then says, "I'm getting a divorce." No one ever starts out to do that. Divorce happens. But Jesus said, "He would give us beauty for ashes." You really need to build new traditions for your blended family. Children remember how the family used to be. Now, the family, as they knew it is no more. So when you come into a blended family, try to start some new fun traditions. My step-daughter, Tiffany, is grown now. She has her own child now. Her mother didn't want her to call me mom. That was fine with me. So they called me mammy.

One of the traditions we started was having cookie parties at Christmas time. We would have the cousins and friends over. It's a fun tradition we started. This past year we didn't have a cookie party because of a heavy schedule. I thought that of all people the one who would be bummed out about it would be Cassidy, our youngest daughter. But it was Tiffany. She said to me the other day, "Mammy, can we please have a cookie party next year? I want to keep that tradition going." It meant a great deal to them, and I didn't even realize how much.

Birthdays are a good tradition-starter day. We always slip into the birthday person's bedroom in the middle of the night or early in the morning and tie balloons on the person's toes. When they wake up in the morning, we stand there with silly string, and we shoot them all over with it.

We do crazy stuff. We made a tradition of carving pumpkins at Halloween time. When the children's father would come home, then the fun really began. Now I'm a meticulous housekeeper and I don't like messes, but on Halloween we have fun. I give in to the mess phobia. When Daren comes home, as soon as he walks through the kitchen door, we throw the insides of the pumpkin at him. It is so much fun! We work on doing fun things with our family. Our oldest daughter, Tiffany, values these traditions. They mean so much to her.

The Jealousy is JUNK!

Proverbs 27:4 CEV *An angry person is dangerous, but a jealous person is even worse.*

Laura: Let me just say something to step-parents. You need to get over yourself. If you have a problem with jealousy, then don't get married to a man that has children. The same goes to a man, if you have a problem with jealousy – don't get married to a woman with children. You see, the two becoming one is difficult. The Bible says, "A man shall leave his father and mother, be united to his wife and the two become one." The becoming one part takes on a whole new level when you're in a blended family. You really have to prepare to let a lot of things go.

It really brings peace in a child to speak well of his or her mother or father. I'm not a perfect person, believe me. I have my faults. While Daren and I were dating and when we first got married, Tiffany and Cami constantly talked about their mother. At first I thought, "Oh, please quit." It would go on and on. Finally, I came to the place where I had to ask myself, "Do I tell them how much it bothers me and ask them to stop?" After I thought about it, I realized it was ridiculous. Children should be able to talk about their parents. I decided to go with it. I worked on overcoming the pain and insecurity I was feeling at the beginning of our marriage. I allowed the children talk about their mother.

How sad and painful it would've been to prevent them from talking about their mother. I had to dig deep. I decided to fall in love with these children, with all my heart, and love their mother, too. I did that. I found qualities that I liked about her, and focused on them. She's a hard worker. She is wonderful to the children. I would talk about those qualities to the girls. It bonded us.

Rather than dogging the ex, find the good qualities about them. Honor them in front of the children. It will endear them to you. I chose to do that. It wasn't easy at first. But you are the adult. You have to grow up and be the responsible party in this. Even if the children have very bad behavior, don't get on the same level as the child. You be the mature one. Bite your lip. Be the adult. Even if things aren't going your way, be like Jesus to them. That's how the world looks at us and sees or doesn't see Christ in us. When we act like Christ, the world takes note of that. We shouldn't act like a carnal person. We don't return evil for evil. We have the power within us to overcome those things.

Daren: Going back to jealousy, one thing Laura is very good at is honoring the good traits in the girls' mother. One of the most destructive things in life is jealousy. If it's going to show up anywhere, it will show up in this area of exes, ex-husbands, and ex-wives. Just make a commitment to junk jealousy. Don't allow yourself to be a jealous person. You can be jealous over so many things. People can be jealous of what kind of car a person drives, where they live, how much money they make, who they're married to, or who they use to be married to – junk the jealousy.
Jealousy is very destructive. I repeat, the Bible says this about jealousy.
Proverbs 27:4 TEV *Anger is cruel and destructive, but it is nothing compared to jealousy.*

In another translation:
Proverbs 27:4 CEV *An angry person is dangerous, but a jealous person is even worse.*

One of the worst things you can do is allow jealousy to be part of your life. We have a policy at our church that concerns jealousy. If we spot any form of jealousy in a person's life, then that person is not allowed a leadership position until the jealousy is out of their life. One of most destructive things to a family, to a church or any organization is jealousy. If you have a jealous person in the midst, they will surely ruin it for everybody else.

Don't Stress

A foundational scripture for the blended family is...
Ephesians 4:32 *"Be kind to one another, tenderhearted, forgive one another, even as God for Christ sake hath forgiven you."*

When a crisis happens, these typical things happen. Most people will initially blame someone, and then personally attack their integrity or motives. This scripture is the antidote for dealing with the stress that goes on between an ex-wife or ex-husband, and then the stress that exists with your existing spouse. I mean, this can be a nest of stress! A typical marriage is stressful enough, let alone a blended family, with all the added stress factors coming into play. This can get really crazy – so you have to make up your mind that you are going to put God first. You have to decide early on that you're going to live by Biblical principles. You choose to apply scriptures like Ephesians 4:32. You work at being kind to one another. You make a quality decision to be tender, even when you are upset. The temptation, when crisis hits, is to start blaming and finger pointing. Any time there is trouble, our human response is to point a finger and say, "It's her fault/ his fault/ your fault." Blaming someone else is a typical response.

Another thing we worked on diligently was scheduling a weekly conference time. This can prevent heated arguments – and nothing is resolved from such heated debates. I learned this one from my dad and mom. Dad said, "Look, when you have ongoing issues that need to be resolved – schedule an appointment with one another." We discovered that defuses all the whining, complaining and off-the-cuff anger. You make it civilized. You say, "Ok, we have differences of opinion. Let's come together and make a list of things we want to talk about – and write down why we feel the way we feel about them." We would meet Thursday after work. We would treat it very respectfully and look forward to the meeting. We would sit down with our notes in front of us. And we would have a civil conversation. There were times we just didn't agree. There still are.

There were some issues in our marriage, concerning the girls, where Laura had her opinions and I had mine. We would talk and talk. We went through a couple of those issues for years. She would pray for me, "Lord, help this man, he is really not getting it. I know I'm right. I know he's really messed up. Please let him come to the place where he agrees with me." She would pray that way over and over – year after year. We finally decided that we were going to agreeably disagree. There are some issues you may never agree on. But you can really be happy anyway.

We get in trouble when we feel like the only time we can be happy is when everyone is in agreement. That's unrealistic. We are different individuals. We believe the Word, but some things are gray areas that are not necessarily sin. We can have a difference of opinion in a few of these areas. Laura said, "Ok, you know what, they're your girls. You're the head of the household, I'm just submitting my will to you and I'm going to be happy about it." Now you know that took work – because she really didn't want to be happy about it. In her mind, she knew she was right and she believed I needed to agree with her. But she did get happy. As time went by, I did start seeing a few things her way, and she saw a few things my way. The key was agreeing to disagree. When dealing with issues we made a deal: don't sweep them under the rug.
Ephesians 4:15 *Instead, speaking the truth in love.*

Think before you speak. Once words leave your mouth, it is impossible to drag them back. Be quick to listen and slow to speak.
Proverbs 13:3 *He who guards his lips guards his life, but he who speaks rashly will come to ruin.*

Proverbs 4:24 *Put away perversity from your mouth; keep corrupt talk far from your lips.*

In some conflicts, you come to the point where you say, "This is not worth the conflict." You learn to pick your battles. Not all things are worth fighting over. One of the best things you can do to avoid conflict is to think before you speak. It can be hard to do! Typically, we quickly react and the poison flies out. Once those words leave your mouth, it is impossible to retrieve them. Be quick to listen and slow to speak.

I suppose that when you have conflict and crisis, one of the best gifts you can give another human being is to put yourself in their shoes. Even if you are one hundred percent certain that you are right, develop the ability to put yourself in their situation and their shoes. Try to honestly see the issue from their perspective. The problem with most of us is that we think if we put ourselves in their shoes, we're admitting that we might be wrong. We don't want to see it their way because they're screwed up. Do yourself a favor – open your mind. Pray.

Here is an example of a prayer that might work for you:

"OK, God. I will stand with my core values here. I believe them and I'm committed to them. In order that I might reach them and communicate with them, I'm going to try to see life the way they are seeing it for a minute. Please open my eyes so that I can understand why they see the situation like as they do. Bless us both, Lord"

Being able to create a safe and sacred space where you can meaningfully work through issues is a great gift. It's also a sign of maturity. What you're saying when you do that is, "I'm secure with my opinion and my beliefs. I am secure with who I am." Looking at life through your messed up point of view doesn't mean I'm going to be messed up. It's a great ability to develop. You may even change your mind in the process of exercising this ability.

Let me share this truth with you. Things go better if you focus on the good things. This will help your family with any conflict you might be going through. A blended family is definitely vulnerable to times of conflict. But things get messed up in any family. I have a seventeen year old son who is eating us out of house and home. So we deal with our own issues. Laura said to me, "Have the talk." She meant something different than I heard. I sat my son down and had "the talk." I said, "The first and most important thing to realize is that there are five other people in this house besides you. We all feel like we are in competition for the food in this house." When all you see is the problem, and all you focus on is what's wrong, you miss the point.

Stop looking for the negative. Change your perspective. Change your focus. Although it's not easy, and you won't always feel like doing this, if you do, your feelings will come into alignment. Get a piece of paper and begin to make a list of all the things that are right and good. I promise you, that you'll be able to come up with at least five good things immediately. By the time you get to five, you'll be able to name another five. Now you have ten things that are good in your relationship and in your life. Start simple. For example, the fact that you can both breathe is a good thing. You can see, smell, taste, and so on. Write down the things you are thankful for.

The next thing you can do is make a vision board. What is a vision board? A vision board is a picture board that reminds you of what you want. What is it that you want? Decide what you want to accomplish and make a list of things you want to purchase – like a new car. Perhaps you want your marriage to be better. Have a vision board for every member of your family, including your kids, and don't forget about yourself.

Finally, be mentally thankful and aware every time you refer back to your vision board. When negative feelings come, when you start to think about what's wrong, when you begin to feel doubtful or gloomy about your future, get out your list. Reread twelve or fifteen things and keep your heart and mind on the vision. This will eventually change the way you feel. When you begin to feel the difference, then you'll begin to act different. The way to change your actions and behaviors is to change your thoughts. Start thinking differently. Keep your eyes and heart on where you're going.
Look away from where you've been. That change in thinking will produce new actions, which will bring a full life and many blessings to you. That is what the Word says.

II Corinthians 5:7 *"We live by faith, not by sight."*

Here is another prayer that can be really helpful:
"Heavenly Father, I pray for every family, blended or not, son, daughter, step-parent, step-children, all marriages. Lord, I pray you would just knit hearts together. Draw all of our family members together, closer than ever before. I pray you would heal hurts and help people to forgive and move forward in their lives. I pray in Jesus name, amen."

CHAPTER 4
FOUR Wrongs Make a Right

Is Peace Possible?

Conflict is inevitable in a marriage. I've learned that when you're in the middle of a crisis and it seems like things are going south, one of the best things you can do is get outside of crisis for the moment. Sometimes that may be for only half an hour at a time – sometimes it may be several hours. Occasionally, you'll want to get outside of the crisis for a full day. That doesn't mean you go to bed angry. It does mean you have peace and take a break from it. Hopefully the break isn't too long. But we need some time out so we cool our emotions down, so we can come back together and talk about things in a cool, calm, collected manner.

Scripture reminds us to never go to bed angry.
Ephesians 4:26 NKJV *"Be angry, and do not sin": do not let the sun go down on your wrath*

You don't want to go to bed with an angry, jealous or sickened heart. So what do you do when you have unresolved issues at bed time? You simply say, "You know what? We will talk about this later." My wife especially likes this scripture. She's the type of person who likes to resolve everything immediately. She struggles sometimes, especially in the middle of a conflict. I personally don't like confrontation, particularly about issues that I could possibly be wrong about. But I've grown in this area, and my wife has grown in this area, too. We finally figured out how this works. She used to insist that we resolve everything right away and talk about it. From my wife's perspective, men just need some time to think about the issue. Her thinking is that men don't think as quickly as women, and therefore they need more time to figure it out. So she learned to give me space and time. She claims it didn't work very well for several years. An hour would go by, maybe a day would go by – two days would go by. In the meantime, she's waiting on me to come back and deal with the issue. And I'm not coming back.

Because of this, my wife suffered a lot of turmoil. Then the adversary, the enemy of our soul, lies to you. Satan, the father of all lies, says, "He doesn't care. He doesn't care about your feelings. This isn't important to him." Outwardly she seemed all calm, but in the back of her mind she was dwelling on the fact that I wasn't coming back to talk about it. Millions of thoughts would go through her head, until ultimately, she would just snap. This whole concept just didn't work well at first. I finally disciplined myself to just come back and talk about it. I made myself talk about it. What that did was bring her peace and increased her trust, knowing that even if things got intense and heated, we would have that moment in time, when we would discuss it. As long as she knew that a time would come when we would discuss the issue and she would have opportunity to share her perspective, then the concept of taking a break worked well. It works so well now that we both have significantly improved in managing our anger.

My wife and I have had a couple of issues we could never come to terms with. During our whole marriage we never solved them. We finally said, 'These issues will be solved as time goes by and the girls grow up and move out on their own." You may have issues like that. You must not hold those issues against one another. You won't budge, she won't budge, but you finally have to say at the end of the day, "I love you anyway." It takes maturity to do that, but it makes for a really peaceful life. Life can be hard with all the things we have to deal with outside of the marriage. Home should be a refuge, a place of peace, a place of fun. Strife should be low to none. Work through issues to come to a resolution. Don't just fight. Children want to come home and enjoy being with their mom and dad.

When we came to the conference table and dealt with heated issues in an amiable manner, our trust developed beyond our imagination. Now we really trust each other. We know that we love each other enough to come back and deal with the issues. Before we figured this out, my wife misjudged me, not realizing I simply don't like conflict. However, I want issues resolved as much as she does. I would shut down because she was so angry. She learned how not to be angry. I learned how not to shut down. Now we always come back to the conference table. We honestly get along very well now. We hardly ever have a conflict. We are not a bickering couple. It's a wonderful way to live.

Mad Men (and women)
There's an important scripture in Proverbs that deals with anger.
Proverbs 22:24-25 NKJV *Make no friendship with an angry man, And with a furious man do not go, 25 Lest you learn his ways*
And set a snare for your soul.

If you grew up in an angry home, a strife-filled home, you no doubt picked up some patterns of thought and conflict that you've got to break. If your parents were "yellers," then that is probably something that you struggle with. Learn to speak without shouting. Make a conscious decision to behave in a disciplined way, just like on a diet, or a person who is quitting smoking. You have the power in God to break those patterns. The way you break this is to learn to yield to the Holy Spirit in those moments. When we don't get our way, we need to be able to shut our mouth and yield to the Holy Spirit.

Part of our maturing in Christ is learning to manage our emotions. The longer I walk with the Lord, the more He has His finger on this area of my life. He will not let my emotions go unchecked. What is so interesting is that the longer you walk with Him, the more He helps you manage your joy. You know you're moving into the realm of maturity in Christ when He starts helping you manage your joy in the midst of conflict and touchy issues. What I mean is, you control your joy by controlling your thinking.

Here's an idea that I heard once and it is really effective: When your spouse is so angry with you that they've gone into another room, maybe even to bed without resolving the issue, then you should find it inside of yourself to just let it go for one minute. Go into the other room where your spouse is and just hug them. Give your spouse one giant, wordless hug. Remember how much that person loves you and how much you love them, just for a moment. It will make discussing the problem so much easier and will keep you from sitting and telling yourself how awful the other person is behaving. In so many areas of life, being the one who can let go is such a virtue.

The way you control your thinking is to go back and deliberately think about what is right. That's why you need to make your gratitude list. It will help you manage your emotions. When your emotions are whacked out, you have feelings that cause you to start thinking.
"Why am I doing this? Why are we in this? I don't want to see him. I don't want to see her."

Your emotions can get out of control so easily. If you've been meditating on your list of good things, you are attracted and drawn those things. That's why a person who thinks lustful thoughts feels lust. Their whole life begins to go in that direction. Whatever gets your attention gets you. Whatever captures your thought life will determine the direction of your life.

Plan B (and D and E and Z)
Planning in advance and giving thought to future possibilities is a great help to the blended family. A wife or a husband who has the ability to look down the road and see what may be coming is a tremendous asset. My wife is very gifted in this area. This looking ahead process can bring genuine peace. Simple basic life principles, like discipline and knowing God's order of things, can help tremendously. If you are an undisciplined person – not reading your Bible, or spending time in prayer or attending church – you'll come up short with

spiritual resources to deal with blended or un-blended family issues. Dealing with exes, financial issues, children and step children will tax you to the limit. Marriage itself is challenging. Knowing God's way of doing things is so much easier when you have an ongoing healthy relationship with Christ. When you love God, you automatically begin to live your life through the Spirit and live God's way.

It's not just black and white.
"OK, the Husband is the head of the household."

I've known couples who have this going on. A sweet, intimate relationship with the Lord will prevent the legalistic 'do's and 'don'ts from entering the picture. The Apostle Paul, in writing his letter to the Ephesian church, tells us what God's order of marriage is. The world has all kinds of crazy ideas about this and has really lost a lot of respect for the institution, but God hasn't changed. His plan remains the same.

Ephesians 5:21-24 NLT *And further, you will submit to one another out of reverence for Christ.* ²² *You wives will submit to your husbands as you do to the Lord.* ²³ *For a husband is the head of his wife as Christ is the head of his body, the church; he gave his life to be her Savior.* ²⁴ *As the church submits to Christ, so you wives must submit to your husbands in everything.* ²⁵ *And you husbands must love your wives with the same love Christ showed the church.*

God is saying that this mystery of marriage, the two becoming one, is like Christ's marriage to the church. Knowing this order, and knowing that it is God's way, brings a real peace to the marriage. It's not a dictatorial, one sided relationship. It's a mutual submission to one another in the Spirit that brings forth lasting peace. This mutual submission to one another gives a Godly order to the home. Husbands and wives following Christ after the Spirit never use scripture to get their way. They honestly listen to one another.

Ephesians 5:28-32 NLT *In the same way, husbands ought to love their wives as they love their own bodies. For a man is actually loving himself when he loves his wife. ²⁹ No one hates his own body but lovingly cares for it, just as Christ cares for his body, which is the church. ³⁰ And we are his body. ³¹ As the Scriptures say, "A man leaves his father and mother and is joined to his wife, and the two are united into one." ³² This is a great mystery..."*

We must listen to one another as close friends. A great marriage is the result of a great friendship. When your best friend is your spouse, you're well on your way to a fabulous marriage. It is so important to have that friendship. How does mutual submission work with best friends when they are husbands and wives? After you have a lot of discussion – not asking one another to do something contrary to the Word of God – and it's not a matter of sin – it's just a matter of opinion. You've been through the tunnel and talked everything out. It's a matter of opinion and a household decision. If it's a serious thing, I say, "I'm going to trust the Lord with this. I may not agree with your point of view, but I'm going to trust the Lord with you." There it is again. Faith and submission to God's will. You have to have faith. You will see that it just keeps popping up again and again.
There will be times when one of you will say, "You know, I think you're right on this." I *never* say, "Hey, I'm the head of the house and this is the way it's going to be." Your wife is never to be a little subservient slave. That is not God's intention.

Conflicting Stories
Men and women deal with conflict differently. It's funny, because men and women expect each other to understand, think, and feel the same way they do. This is part of why I used to avoid conflict early in my marriage. When I say that the one thing I've learned in eighteen years of marriage is that a happy wife makes a happy life, I mean it! It is a true statement! Men, those of you who are married already know this truth. Here's why. The number one thing a man wants in

his home is peace. If there is conflict going on between him and his wife, he becomes insecure. He hates it. He wants to bury his head in the sand. He wants to avoid it at all cost. He wants it to go away. If this is how a grown, strong man feels, then can you imagine how a child might feel during a time of conflict in the home? They are instantly insecure about everything.

 We want peace above just about anything else. If we have a long extended period of tension and no peace, we start to pull away. We pull away until we eventually go into our own little world and become withdrawn, protective and defensive. Eventually, a man adapts to that environment, and you'll never be able to get through to him. He seals himself off into a cocoon-like existence.

Listen to what Proverbs says about this:
Proverbs 17:1 *"A dry crust eaten in peace is better than steak everyday along with argument and strife."*

That is a scripture all men can relate to. Men would rather have bread and water than steak with a fight. (And if you don't have a happy wife, then all that you have to eat might just be bread and water!) Men just don't like conflict. But here's what I've learned about women: women deal with issues differently. Men are goal oriented, women are process oriented. It's through the process of talking about it that women deal with conflict. I don't know why God did this, but as women process, they get angrier and more upset. My wife says, "It is passion, honey, passion." I say passion is a good cover for anger. It sounds better. It dresses up the issue. But what really happens is, as men, we don't want to go through that tunnel of conflict because it's painful for us. Did I say that I've learned this? What I meant is that I'm learning this; I have not arrived yet. My wife says I'm a lot better than I used to be. She says that I look at her now, instead of looking all around. I don't leave the house so that she has to follow me all over to hear my point of view. I'm getting better.

In the first years of our marriage, she'd follow me around until I finally just walked out the door and there I'd go. It was so painful for her. I've realized that if I can dodge the bullets for just a little while, it'll work out. I've learned that as a woman processes her intensity goes up. The longer that you let her *think*, the worse that the wrath will be. A marriage counselor told me I needed to communicate, to talk. But when I tried to do it, there was hell to pay! It got worse – for a little while. What we can learn to do as men is to suck it up and dodge the bullets when they come. Just listen. Don't get defensive.

Dodging the bullets and listening doesn't give the wife a license to sin. The Bible clearly says, "You can be angry and not sin." How you communicate that anger is so important. Knowing how to fight right is a must for couples. When you point fingers and accuse, you automatically shut the other person down. They will always get defensive on you. They will not hear what you're saying. You have to learn how to word things.

Laura: I'd say, "Ok, I got the book out, read my marriage retreat materials and I'll try not to blame." I would do it all by the book, and he would still have a spasm. I'd say to myself, "What is the deal? We didn't curse or scream at each other." But what he was learning was to sit there and go through the process with me. It's so difficult for a man to do that. He learned to detach and tell himself, "OK, she's upset. She has a right to her emotions. She has a right to feel this way. She has a desperate need to be heard."

Daren: I've learned to listen and let her talk through the process even if I think she's wrong. There were times when I would allow her to just talk' and as I listened she would occasionally come to a satisfactory resolution on her own. (Don't tell her that I said that…)

Women have so many female friends because they desperately need someone to talk to. They need to talk. Women will let each other talk and say the craziest things. In their minds they may be thinking, 'She's wrong,' but they'll never say it – they just let her talk. How much greater that is when it's your spouse sitting and listening to what you're saying – even if they think you're wrong – they let you say it. A person feels validated and valued when you listen to them.

I want to tell you something about myself. The hardest thing in the world for me to do is sit still and listen when I feel blame coming my way. When we deal with issues, I feel like I'm getting blamed if you're bringing it up to me. But that's not necessarily true. Men are problem solvers. I feel like God wired me to solve problems. So I have to learn to sit back and listen – let her process.

What a man needs is affirmation. Ladies, you can get a lot of mileage out of a few compliments because we men have huge little-boy egos. We are really just living our life for the next compliment. I'm letting you in on one of man's most hidden secrets. We husbands live our life for the approval of our wives. As a pastor, one of the first things I do when I get home after church is to subtly ask my wife, "What did you like about the service?" She usually doesn't wait for me to ask. She usually says something good. She doesn't lie about it. She always finds the good and makes positive comments, which makes me feel great.

Listen to how the Amplified Bible addresses this in Ephesians:

"However let each man of you, without exception, love his wife as being in a sense, his very own self, and let the wife see that she respects and reverences her husband, that she notices him, regards him, honors him, prefers him, venerates and esteems him and that she defers to him, praises him, and loves and admires him exceedingly."

Do think God is trying to get a point across? This passage goes on and on. And then He likens the marriage to the relationship of Christ and the church. What does God demand? He demands honor, praise, respect, and to love Him above all others. He wants to be the center of our life. He's the one who is saying our marriage is like Christ and the church. Ladies, read it in the Amplified Bible. When you give your husband honor, respect and love, he will automatically want to lay his life down for you.

We see so many times in broken homes and painful relationships self-centered narcissistic people. Neither the wife nor the husband is laying their life down for the other. The wife is not respecting, honoring and loving her husband. The husband does not love his wife as he should. They are locked in this self-centered, vicious cycle of butting heads, rather than saying, "You know what, I'm going to let her talk, respect her and love her." Believe me, sometimes it is laying your life down when you have to sit and listen to a woman dealing with issues. A woman can go on and on and on. But men, it's important to listen-until she is finished. The question always in the man's mind is, '*When* will she be done?' Ha!

A woman will love, honor and respect a man who takes the time to listen to her. The reason I'm touching on this in the blended family is because this is foundational, this is basic to having a meaningful relationship. Without having some basic marital values and principles operating in your relationship and with all the added multiplied dimensions that a blended family brings to the table, your chances of surviving are much more problematic than in your first marriage. The divorce rate on the blended family is sixty-five percent. This fact, I believe is a result of the increased difficulty of blending our past with our present as it relates to our new family.

Learning to Love

I use to bum out because I'd hear this teaching from the scripture, "Men, love your wives." And you know it tells women to respect their husbands. Finally one day I found in the book of Titus, "Teach women to love their husbands."

Titus 2:4 *"Train the younger women to love their husbands and children, to be self controlled and pure, to be busy at home and to be kind and to put their own husbands first, so that no one can say insulting things about the word of God.*

The scripture goes on and on about how we are to defer to and prefer the opposite spouse. Love the other person first. In the first few years of marriage, you may be defensive and protective. In fact, you can go a whole lifetime in that mode. It's when we learn to say to ourselves, "You know what, things are going to be ok, I do not have to defend myself." It's not as big of a deal as I thought it was. Aren't some of things you used to fight over silly? It's embarrassing to think about them now. We've had arguments at a drive-through at McDonalds. She would write the order down to make it easier for me, and I'd still get it wrong. I had a one hundred percent track record of failure. Finally, she would go herself or say, "Honey, don't worry about it." It just wasn't worth losing your peace over. It was just ridiculous. Stuff that meant so much to me, like having everything neat and tidy, I learned to let go of. We've come a long way.

We've learned to say, "Oh, well." Little things don't really matter. In the beginning of the marriage, you think that everything matters, and it doesn't. I have a phrase, '*It don't matter.*" Really, some things just don't matter.

You have to choose your battles. Not everything is worth fighting over. Some things *are* worth going to war over. Those things are your core values. When those are violated, you must speak up. Our children, Tiffany and Cami, are twenty- three and twenty- one now. It seemed like they would always be young. It seemed like their problems would never go away. It seemed like the child support would never go away. But eventually, they grew up and we were left with each other. It is not that we resented the child support at all, but it was for us present during very financially difficult times. Sometimes you feel like this stuff will never go away, will never change. But your children will grow up, move out and go out on their own. So you have to work on your relationship.

Are You Listening to Me?

There are so many things that my wife tells me that I know that I never, ever heard. I'm not sure how that is possible, but somehow there are things which are said, and it's like they disappear the minute that they enter my ears. It's as if there is an extra part of my brain that just sucks up certain conversations and turns them to dust! I'm wasn't being disrespectful or mean and I wasn't *not* listening; but somehow I just immediately forgot. Men, women just want us to hear them out. Learn to listen to them. Try to understand them. Put yourself in their shoes. This will help you immensely in your relationship. Try to see their point of view, to see things from their perspective and then reflect it back to them. They'll know that you heard them and you understood them. It will mean more to them than you can imagine. Even if you don't agree with them, it will mean so much to them.

Women love to be cherished. God made them to be cherished. God actually calls them the weaker vessel, not in the sense of being inferior, but in the sense of being more valuable and fragile. A woman is very valuable. She is strong in character. She is a multi-tasker. She has a tendency to be emotionally based, while a man is not. A woman has different needs.

1 Peter 3:7 *"Husbands in the same way, be considerate as you live with your wives, treat them with respect as the weaker partner and as heirs with you of the precious gift of life so that nothing will hinder your prayers.*

The Bible actually tells us that a wrong relationship with our spouse will hinder our prayer life. So we have to love, respect and cherish our spouse. When we operate in that avenue of love our prayers are heard. The Bible goes on to say, *"Live in harmony with one another, all of you, be sympathetic, loving, compassionate, and humble. Don't repay evil with evil or insults with insults, but blessings."* When someone has done you wrong, you should bless them because of this spiritual truth. Remember you will inherit a blessing.

Let me tell you women, we men never ignore happiness. If you want to keep your husband from having roving eyes, let him always see a happy wife. What happens so often with men out in the marketplace or at work is that they think, "Can I make her happy or could I make her happy?" The true bottom line in the relationship is, 'Can I keep you happy?' That's really spiritual, isn't it? I'm just telling you the way guys think, ok? There are certain things that happen to a man and a woman before they walk out on each other. God made men to take in, and He made women to give out. A man wants to know if he can make you happy and keep you happy. Here's what a man says when he gets ready to walk out on a woman, "I can't make her happy, no matter what I do. I've tried everything I know, and I can't make her happy."

On the other hand, when a woman walks out on a man, she says, "I have given and given. I've done all that I can. I don't have any more to give. I'm done. I've given all I can and it makes no difference."

I'm not trying to magnify your problems. I'm just sharing some things with you that will help you get on the right track. I'm not just teaching about marriage. I'm letting you in on our personal life and personal testimony. Hopefully out of our testimony, your marriage can grow and become better.

No matter how good or bad your marriage might be, it can improve.

Make a List

Here's a list of things that will improve your relationship with your wife:

1. Purposeful communication. Make eye contact when she's talking and really listen to what she's saying.

2. Appreciate and respect differences.

3. Give up judgments. When we feel we are right, we become the judge and jury, and declare the sentence. One of the most peaceful things you can do is cease to judge. Your wife (or husband) doesn't need to be judged. Many times we think we know why a person is doing something or we think we understand their behavior. It may have nothing to do with

what we think. We can assume so much. And we can make so many mistakes when we are assuming. Keep your mind open. Don't assume you know everything.

4. Accept responsibility. This is such a key to having a good relationship. This is simply saying, *"I'm sorry." "I was wrong." "I was inconsiderate."*

5. Practice forgiving. Learn to be a great forgiver. If you are a Christian, you love the way He loves and forgive the way He forgives. Scripture teaches us that we are forgiven the way we forgive.

6. Buy her little gifts for no special reason. Women love that. Men like words. Women like things.

I want to share some great insights about parenting and children with you in the next chapter.

CHAPTER 5
FIVE Star Family Values

What Values will Make this Family Work?

I received a letter this week from a little girl named Lisa who attends my church. The letter was to thank me for talking about blended families during my sermon. She just so happens to be a part of one, and the topic really hit home for her. Just when you think that the little ones aren't listening, you find out that they hear everything.

It may seem to you that Laura and I talk about the blended family like we have all the solutions. It may seem that way to you, but I want to tell you, we don't. We are just sharing with you what we've learned through our own experiences. We also have thoroughly examined what God's word has to say about the blended family. With the help of God's word and our personal experiences, we've come up with some very valuable solutions for the blended family.

There are so many factors that come into play when you talk about the blended family. You have different levels of maturity in ex-husbands and ex-wives. You have people dealing with jealousy and insecurity. You have some other people dealing with control issues, including the children. All of these factors influence the blended family. If everyone in the blended family were mature, then divorce probably wouldn't have happened in the first place. So there's a lot of immaturity and inappropriate behavior that can trouble a blended family.

One of the things that will really help in your marriage is if your spouse has problems with members of your family, then you deal with your family. For example; if the wife has problems with his family then he should deal with his family, and not make her deal with them. When it comes to blended families, the children should respect the step-parents and they should listen to them and obey then.

Navigating the waters of a blended family is like riding rough rapids. You may think you are going smoothly down the river and all of a sudden you hit the rapids and you're in a level five rough rapid. It's like your life turning upside down and you don't know what to do. But remember what I said before: The beautiful view at the end of the rapids is totally worth the rough ride.

I'm attempting to give you some foundational principles and some practical boundaries that will help you do blended life more successfully. Your goal is not perfection but improving and being a better mother, father, and a child and dealing with the exes in a mature way. That is the way that God would want it to be.

The pivotal point of this whole book is that we have to prioritize our relationships. First on the relationship priority list is our relationship with God. It's God first of all. That's a given. God has to be first in your life.

Second in your relationship priorities is the relationship between a husband and wife. This is the marriage relationship. This foundational truth is fundamental to bringing peace and security to a relationship. The temptation is to put children at the top of the priority list – children really want to be there too. If you think about it though, how can your children learn from your marriage if you are putting them before your spouse? They need to see that loving relationship in your daily life in order to learn from it and hopefully mimic it someday when they get married.

Let me recommend an excellent book for you to read. This is called *KIDS CEO* and it's written by Ed Young, Senior Pastor of Fellowship Church in Dallas Texas. It's a fabulous book dealing with marriage and children. The title is very revealing as children really do want to be the CEO of the Home

Corporation. Parents need to move into executive leadership of the home. Children become support members.
Proverbs 22:15 *'Foolishness is bound in the heart of a child.'*

Why would we give the corner office or the leadership position to a child when they don't even know how to run themselves? Our job is to teach, train and discipline them. We need to be the adult, the one running the family.

I have a friend who got pregnant right out of high school. I hadn't seen her for several years. I went back to my hometown on the 4th of July and went to the local carnival. I ran into her and her husband. They have a beautiful little boy. I was so excited to talk to her, but I only got about two minutes of conversation with her. Her little boy was holding both her hand and her husband's hand. He was so excited about riding the carnival rides that he wouldn't allow his mom and dad to talk with me.

Proverbs 22:6 NKJV *Train up a child in the way he should go, And when he is old he will not depart from it.*

So he proceeded to kick, first his mom, then his dad. Kick, kick, and instead of correcting him, they both leaned over in leg pain and said, "Well I guess we have to go." I thought to myself, "That child has been trained." Children sometimes end up training us, but it should be us training the child. That made such an impression on my mind. I didn't have children at the time. I thought oh my goodness. I do not want my children to run my home like that.

When we talk about priorities, your first priority and loyalty goes to your wife, even over your biological children. I know that goes against the grain of our feelings sometimes, but your loyalty goes to your spouse. Wives, your loyalty goes to your husband, even above your biological children. I know that grates on some of you. Remember this: your children will grow up one day and leave home. You continue on with your spouse. The best gift you can give to your children is giving your loyalty to your spouse. Model for them a biblical husband-wife relationship. One common denominator of children from broken homes is the victim mentality. They feel like they've been robbed or cheated of a normal life; and they have. So the best thing you can do in a blended family is say, "I love my spouse and I'm committed to them." That gives your children great security.

Husbands and wives, be worthy of the loyalty your spouse gives you. I mean by that, be mature. Behave properly and accordingly to one another, because you have to earn respect; it's not automatically given. You make it very difficult if you're a step father or step mother preferring your child over your spouse. When you're showing more preference and respect to you biological child than to your spouse, you're not being worthy of your husband or wife's respect – it's not mature behavior being shown, and your child will figure out the situation and use it time and time again in order to control different situations.

Also, if you're treating your children better than you're treating your step children, then you are crossing the line. It makes it so difficult for you and your spouse to be a united couple when dealing with the children. Parents need to love their children and step children equally, with the same love and respect. The other parent will not feel like they have to protect their child from you when you do that. When a wife or husband feels like they have to protect their children from you, you are destined for difficulty.

Respect the Fun
When it comes to discipline, the primary disciplinarian in the family should be the biological parent. Even if he or she is gone, the step parent is there, and those children should be taught to respect and obey him or her. It's very important that the children learn respect. With Tiffany and Cami, they never talked disrespectful to Laura. There were issues with the girls, but they respected her. Respect was something I worked on from day one. The marriage was the first priority. Even our

biological children, Adam, Joel and Cassidy are very respectful. Respect for parents is a big part of the values that cause a young man and woman to grow up and become good parents themselves.

Another great thing you can do for your children is make your house a fun house. Sure, routine and structure are necessary, but not to the exclusion of a fun loving atmosphere. A fun loving environment creates better emotional responses. Great things can be accomplished by just doing silly stuff once in a while. Let me give you an example of what I mean. I called a friend and asked him to help me video tape a bedtime fun event at our house. This is a bedtime tradition we have with Cassidy. We do this every night. We pretend to fill her up with helium gas and then ask her to see how high she can jump. With each jump I lift her higher and higher until finally she lands in bed. It's a lot of fun.

We do some crazy stuff at our house. This week we had a birthday at our house. So we had what we call a SILLY STRING DAY, like I told you about in the last chapter. Adam, our oldest boy, went from sixteen to seventeen. The one who was most excited about the silly string was Cassidy. Cassidy was turning seven at the time of this writing.
She was saying, "Oh yes. I want to go with you to buy the silly string." We bought extra silly string so each person could have two in each hand.
Adam, who was seventeen at the time of this writing, was probably a little too old for silly string. (At least he thought that he was too old.) We silently went down-stairs early in the morning and, sure enough, Adam had a sign on his door – PLEASE DO NOT SILLY STRING ME THIS YEAR (like he was a lot older now). Well, the game was on then! He'll never outgrow family tradition.
Needless to say, he wasn't very happy with us. But he got over it. He will always remember that. I don't want our kids to remember strife, arguments and tension. I want our kids to remember fun times in the home. We all have good memories and bad memories of home life. One of the easiest ways of

making good memories is to lighten up on life. Things really aren't all that bad. There's a lot to be thankful for. We only got one chance to celebrate that moment, and it was totally worth any teenage drama that it may have caused.

Adam has also now reached an age where he has started eating us out of house and home. He is seventeen now and is growing like crazy. He's taller than me now. I wear cowboy boots sometimes just to be able to look him in the eye at eye level. Here's how bad it was, we found that Cassidy was hiding food in her bedroom chest of drawers. Then I realized Laura and I were starting to hide food in our room too. We were training our kids by example. Our other son, Joel, was hiding food too. We needed an intervention. We would go in our bedroom at night and lock the door and eat our food. We were just snacking. We do make it fun in our family. Finally, I had to have a talk with him. I said, "Adam, there are four other people that live in this house besides you. We all feel like we are in competition for food. I read this scripture to him;

Genesis 2:24 *"For this reason (food) a man will leave his father and mother and be united to his wife, and they two shall become one flesh."*

God says you're leaving Adam; for this reason you got to get your own wife and buy your own food. I'm saying that because of two reasons. One, we like to have fun. Two our whole reason for parenting is not to become best friends with our children, but to prepare them for the leaving of our nest. The whole purpose for parenting is to train them and teach them for the day they leave. They should become responsible adults having found their place and purpose in life.
The purpose and process of parenting is very clear. Actually you are training your children to be successful adults. You, as a parent, are working your way out of a job. You are not babysitting and putting up with these little creatures that live in your home, causing you stress and strife. And when it's time for them to leave, you just kick them out to make it on their own. We want to prepare them for life.

Prepper-ation

The first thing you teach them is to obey – obey God's Word. You teach them to obey your word as well. You teach them to obey your word and God's Word as the authority in their life until they get out on their own.

Ephesians 6:1 *"Children obey your parents in the Lord, for this is right."*

Now, if you are the type of parent that just follows your child around the house with a Bible and every time they do something wrong, you quote a scripture to them, then you will probably not get through to them.

What we do in our family, to make it fun and help them to understand the why, is to make life a training ground. We take them in the car, when we watch TV, when we go to a restaurant, when we go a movie, when something happens to them at school; we use them all for training and teachable moments. The other day Cassidy and I were watching a kid show and this little girl in this kid show was so disrespectful. Her conversation toward the adults in the show was so rude. Cassidy looked at me and said, "Oh, mommy, she's not being good, she's going to be in trouble." I said, "You know why Cassidy? God says in His Word that children are to honor their father and mother, that their days may be long on the earth." Rebellion that is in the heart of a child that goes unchecked and undisciplined can cause a child to leave this life very early. It is very important that we teach our children to obey the Word of God.

Deuteronomy 6: 5 – 9 *"You shall love the LORD your God with all your heart, with all your soul, and with all your strength. 6 "And these words which I command you today shall be in your heart. 7 "You shall teach them diligently to your children, and shall talk of them when you sit in your house, when you walk by the way, when you lie down, and when you rise up. 8 "You shall bind them as a sign on your hand, and they shall be as frontlets between your eyes. 9 "You shall write them on the doorposts of your house and on your gates."*

This scripture tells us to expose our children to the Word. The Word will help train them to be obedient to God and to us. The other thing the scripture is talking about is we are to train them in the way they are to go. We should be able to look at our children and recognize the gifts and talents in each one of them individually. Do you know that not everybody is going to be good at everything? Some of your children might not be great at school work. You don't want them to quit school early or lighten up their schooling, but you do want to recognize the areas of giftedness that they do have. As you focus on those areas and offer affirmations to your children in those areas, you'll see great development in them. As parents, we are responsible to help our children identify their gifts and talents. We are to teach them that the reason God gave them their particular giftedness and talented abilities is for His Kingdom and His Purpose. Identify your child's gift, his/her bent, their talent and help them relate that giftedness to the local church. Most of us miss that in our life. Many of us never pick up on this until we're in our thirties or more. I often even see people in their fifties, or sixties, sometimes just then realizing and pick up on the fact that the reason they are so good at this, or that; it is because God wants to use their strength's in His Kingdom.

As Christians, our real purpose for life is not just to be school teachers, principals, administrators, managers, truck drivers, plumbers and so on. All that we are and all that we do should be related to how God wants to use us in His Kingdom. The earlier we start teaching our children this truth, the earlier they can start fulfilling God's purpose for their life.

You have to look at your own motivations as to how you are molding your children. Our motivation should be to shape our children according to God's Word. How sad it is when you see parents living vicariously through their children? Parents who lost their own dreams do this. Insecure parents lack the character to raise their children according to Godly principles. Instead of recognizing their child's gifts, they try to make something of their child that resembles what they want the child to be. Children are not here to feed our ego and make us feel better about ourselves. Our children are to do what God called them on this earth to do. Be careful not to steer a child in the direction you want him/her to go because you didn't go there yourself. Steer them in the direction that God wants for them.

When we have the priority of teaching our children to obey God and nurture their relationship with God, the result of that is a young person who has the ability to make wise choices. They are able to make wise decisions on their own. Psalms 25 verifies this principle.

Psalms 25:12 TLB *Where is the man who fears the Lord? God will teach him how to choose the best.*

The by-product of teaching our children to walk with God is the wise decisions that we eventually get to see them make.

To Spank or not to Spank. Is it Punishment or Discipline?

One thing that is so important for parents to know is the difference between punishment and discipline. There is a goal to discipline. Punishment is giving a penalty for an offense or a fault. However discipline is correction that is driven by love. It is teaching and training according to rules and according to the Word. The Bible says that God loves those He corrects. If all we do is punish when our child makes us angry, then there will be no end to it. You have to remember the greater good for the child. I want my child to be successful in life. Sometimes disciplining consistently is a real challenge, especially if your energy level is down. I remember when Cassidy was born. I was forty years old and I didn't have the same energy I had at nineteen. My energy level went way down. I'd find myself letting things go with my youngest simply because I was worn out. I realized that for her good I had to go beyond my feelings. It's easy to let things go, but look beyond to the greater good.

Ephesians 6:4 TLB *And now a word to you parents. Don't keep on scolding and nagging your children, making them angry and resentful. Rather, bring them up with the loving discipline the Lord himself approves, with suggestions and godly advice.*

Sometimes we do lose our temper. On occasions our patience wears thin. We must be ever so careful not to cross the line in these areas. Remember to discipline for the end's sake and not for your anger because they did something to irritate you.

Hebrews 12:11 NASB *All discipline for the moment seems not to be joyful, but sorrowful; yet to those who have been trained by it, afterwards it yields the peaceful fruit of righteousness.*

Let me make this very clear: we are not to punish our children, it's not about punishment. Doing punishment out of anger is a huge mistake. We are to discipline our children.

People often ask me what the Bible says about spanking. Is spanking appropriate or is 'time out' the best way? Now I want to give you a balanced approach to that question. We live in a culture that would like to make it illegal for you to spank your children. The state of California is already taking steps to enact such a law. If you spank out of anger you are most likely abusing the child. We are never to do that. Spanking is an appropriate form of discipline. Spanking is a Biblical principle. When spanking is done in a loving, appropriate way, it is Biblical.

Many in our culture have never had a spanking. Therefore, it is difficult for many to imagine inflicting a little bit of discomfort on the posterior of a child for Biblical discipline. The Bible says it's appropriate. Remember the verse about foolishness in the heart of a child that I showed you earlier? Well, this is what the Bible goes on to say:

Proverbs 22:15 NASB *Foolishness is bound up in the heart of a child; The rod of discipline will remove it far from him.*

Use common sense when applying discipline. First of all, you are not going to spank a newborn baby. But when a growing infant begins to stare you down and says with emphasis, "No!" Then it's time for the little one to learn what that extra padding on his posterior is for. You, in love, can minister a bit of loving correction on that rear end.

Somewhere around the age of nine to thirteen years of age, spanking begins to be inappropriate. So you begin to correct in other ways that are appropriate. Here's a rule of thumb; correction, instruction and training, not punishment, not anger and no violence or abuse. If you can't control yourself, then you shouldn't spank. There are other ways to discipline. My son, Joel, would rather have a spanking than to be grounded. Knowing the differences in your children is important. For Joel, because he loves to play outside, he could be gone from the time he wakes up until time to go to bed. He loves sports. He's athletic. He loves the outdoors. So for him, to ground him for a weekend is absolute torment.

If you have a child who likes to play on the computer all the time, then grounding them is going to get a, "Whatever," response. They would rather be in their room anyhow. They probably don't like going outside. Grounding them will not affect them at all. You have to find the love language of your child. Learn your children. Identify their gifts. Learn how they respond best to discipline. You never discipline every child exactly the same. They are different, unique and their personality causes them to respond differently to discipline. I've had to learn to do something different with each one of our children.

Laura will tell you that the first words of our three children, Adam, Joel and Cassidy, were her first clues to their individual personalities. Adam's first words were no, no and no. I'll tell you about Adam – he always pushed the boundaries. He still does. He was the child who when touching the ornament on the Christmas tree and being told, "No, don't touch that," he would keep his hand there and then he'd push it a little farther. He would break the ornament. After he experienced the consequences of his behavior, he would decide not to do it again. All that was necessary to correct Joel and Cassidy was a look. She never broke an ornament. I'd tell her no, and she would stop most of the time. Joel's first word was ball. That fits his personality. He plays ball all the time. He's outside all the time. Cassidy's first word was Dada. She is so in love with her daddy. She's the biggest daddy's girl I've ever known. Cassidy even called Laura daddy for a season. (and I'm okay with that...)

I've learned that Cassidy worships me. I will give her just about anything she wants. I have the hardest time telling her no. In fact, I was at the store the other day, and she looked up at me with her little girl smile and said, "Can I have this bunny rabbit?" I'm like melting. I turned my head, looked at Cassidy and said, "Cassidy, how can I say no to that?" She said, "That's why I use this smile." It's hard for me to tell her no. I've learned something else: when we become so passionately authentic and in love with God, I have a feeling the He looks at us and says, "I just can't tell those kids no."

When I see competition in a blended family between the siblings, the biological children and the step children, I always think how much that hurts God's heart. They just don't know how much God loves them. There's more than enough love available. Fighting for love isn't necessary. I tell my older children to watch what Cassidy does in relating to me. Take a clue from her. Have a relationship with us because you love us and not for what we can give you. Go out of your way to love your own parents. Model for your children a loving relationship with your parents. This will go a long way with mom and dad and with the Lord also.

I don't think 'Time Out' with younger children works. It works better with adolescent children. Read this scripture:
Proverbs 13:24 NKJV *He who spares his rod hates his son, But he who loves him disciplines him promptly.*

Don't (don't) A contraction of Do Not)

Let me share a few 'DON'TS' with you.
1. Don't lose your temper. This is a no brainier. Work on controlling your emotions.

2. Don't treat children as small adults. Single mothers have a tendency to do this. When they divorce, they might be lonely and frustrated and they make their child their confidante. Children are not ready to be your peer. They are not ready to be your friend. They need you to be their adult. They desperately need you to be an authority in their life that establishes loving boundaries for them. This will give them enormous security.

3. Don't depend too much on your child for companionship. Your sole source of affection and companionship should never be your child. This will place an enormous, unhealthy weight on the child. You need to have some friends. This is a good reason to be involved in a good church. You as a parent having fellowship with adults will be healthy for the child. As your child grows and matures, they'll be able to handle a friendship with you.

4. Don't be inconsistent with your discipline. There is nothing more confusing to a child than getting into trouble one day and then two days later he/she does the same thing and they don't get into trouble.

5. Don't punish.

6. Don't sabotage your child's relationship with you ex-wife or ex-husband. So many times in blended families a parent will do this. They do this to get even, or maybe it comes from bitterness. Maybe they are hurt. Perhaps they are afraid of losing that child to the other adult.

7. Don't use your child as a pawn in the relationship with your ex. This is something that tempts most every blended couple. It's too easy to do this to get back at, control or manipulate the ex-spouse.

8. Don't use your children to gain information. Never ask your child if dad makes more money now; I want to get more child support.

9. Don't transfer your feelings upon your children. Step parents really need to be above this. Just because your child looks or acts a lot like your ex-wife or husband is no excuse to express anger toward them. They may act

like them or look like them, but they are an individual of their own. Never look at them as a reflection of their mother or father. Make a choice to love them as individuals. No two people are exactly alike. Everyone is unique. Celebrate their individuality. They need to feel your unconditional love.

10. Don't convert your own guilt to over-indulgence with your children. Dads deal with this more than moms. In most cases, he only gets the children on weekends. I struggled with guilt as the girls were only with me for four days out of the month. I was so tempted to sweep issues under the rug and not deal with them. However, our natural children would be disciplined for the same behavior. When the girls were with us, it was a challenge. Don't cause your wife or husband to have to deal with children when it's your responsibility. The children will begin to feel the difference in the way they are disciplined and even begin to feel, "Am I not worthy of the same loving boundaries the other children have?"

We all come from different backgrounds and different situations. None of us have the perfect situation. There are a lot of problems that we all face. Some of what I've written may cause you to say, *"Daren, this all sounds good, but you don't understand my situation. My ex-wife or my ex-husband just doesn't cooperate; my kids won't obey; finances are bad, I can't pay all my child support; this is bad, that is bad."* Here's what I want to say to you, "God knows your situation. God is there for you. No matter what you've gone through, what hurt you've experienced, or your own abuses, God is there for you. Maybe you've failed miserably. I want you to know that God will be a father to you. He loves you right where you are. He will be a father to your children. He will be a mother where you fall short. Look at this scripture with me: Isaiah 66:13 TLB *I will comfort you there as a little one is comforted by its mother.*

God says He will comfort you. Those of you who need a mother or who might need a father should look at what the scripture says here:

2 Corinthians 6:18 NKNV *"I will be a Father to you, And you shall be My sons and daughters, Says the LORD Almighty."*
There is one thing we all have in common. We all need healing in our lives. Even if you're in the seemingly perfect family, it's not so perfect. We've all made mistakes. We can use God's healing touch. I'm in that boat – you're in that boat. We are all there together.

Here's another thing we have in common: we all have a savior named Jesus Christ who has paid the price for our sins. He made Himself totally available to us to tap into His Grace, goodness and forgiveness. He doesn't make this requirement, *"IF you fix your life and you get everything perfect, then I'll accept you and start working with you."*
He's so good that God says this about us, *"IF you'll come to me in your messed up situation – if you'll come to me with you habits, with your hurts, with your pain, and with your sins - I'll love you, accept you and forgive you. I'll put you on a path where you need to be going."*

PRAYER: *"Heavenly Father, I pray for everyone reading this – touch their lives – reach out to them and minister to them. Wrap your arms of love and compassion around them right now. I pray they would begin to see the future with hope and great possibilities. Help them to see a bright future with you. I pray they would begin to experience a super-natural touch from you. In Jesus name I pray, amen."*

CHAPTER 6
SIX or More Boundaries

How Setting Boundaries for In-Laws Bring Success.

I want to continue on with children and parenting. Hopefully by now you are getting on the path to successfully bringing your blended family together in unity. I'm not saying I have all the answers. I'm not saying I've unlocked the code. My wife and I have not found the golden grail which holds all of the answers to having a blended family. We are saying that my wife and I, with our blended family, have worked through a lot of things that are noteworthy. There are some things that we are continuing to work through. We have learned some things. We have accomplished some things. We made mistakes, and we've grown from them. I believe you can benefit from our experiences. I want to tell you where we've made some mistakes. We want to share with you our weaknesses. Also, we will tell you where we've had some glowing success. I will do my best to bring God's Word to you as it relates to your family.

When we talk about children and parenting, it can get confusing. Our role as parents is that of training and teaching our children to become independent. Once they are taught and trained, they mature and then they leave us. Having been trained, they are in a position to be successful and obedient to the Lord. The Bible says one of the first priorities of parents is to teach the children to obey. That is the highest priority. Teach them to obey our word and the Word of God. We live in a culture today where many parents don't teach their kids to obey.
This is really apparent if you go out to dinner. Just go in a restaurant and you'll see parents kicked back and the kids running all over the place, jumping in the next booth – causing an unchecked disturbance for everybody around them – throwing paper napkins, spilling ketchup and sugar. My point

is that we should be able to say to our children, "Come over here and sit down," and expect them to obey.

Now not every kid is perfect, and some of them will challenge you. But as parents we ought to have the type of relationship with them where they know that there will be consequences for the disobedience.

My dad could paralyze me and my brothers with nothing but a look. He had the look, man. I could be across the room, and if he gave me the look, a reverential fear gripped my inner soul. Believe me, I was not one of those children who were void of spankings. My dad believed in spankings. My brother Chris (who is three years younger than I am) and I had some memorable spankings. My dad offered up championship spankings. By the time my brother Brian came along (he's ten years younger than I am) my dad was worn out with me and Chris. So Brian has had a gravy train through life. He didn't get many championship spankings.

Here's what I know: we as parents are to train our children to obey. By learning to obey our word, they also learn the importance and practical applications of obeying the Lord. Now I'm talking about balance. I'm not talking about you being a strict, no fun parent. You ought to be fun to be around, but you also need to have that look when it's called for.

In Psalms, David said he was corrected by the look of the Lord. That reminded me of my father. When I was going up, he would look across the room and that look communicated unspoken volumes.

The basis for children growing up is Genesis 2:24

Genesis 2:24 NASB *For this reason a man shall leave his father and his mother, and be joined to his wife; and they shall become one flesh.*

Children are to eventually grow up, mature and leave our homes. There is no other process on planet earth that is more rewarding, more challenging and more expensive than raising children. I believe it's the toughest job we have. It takes more time, more finances and more of our energy than anything else we do. But it also can be extremely rewarding to see our kids grow up and be successful. What really blesses you is to see your children grow up and start making wise decisions, right choices on their own. That is so exciting.

Deuteronomy 6:5-9 NASB *"You shall love the LORD your God with all your heart and with all your soul and with all your might. 6 "These words, which I am commanding you today, shall be on your heart. 7 "You shall teach them diligently to your sons and shall talk of them when you sit in your house and when you walk by the way and when you lie down and when you rise up. 8 "You shall bind them as a sign on your hand and they shall be as frontals on your forehead. 9 "You shall write them on the doorposts of your house and on your gates."*

I believe that this is the foundation for what parenting is all about. The instruction here is to parents, but also to children. Our responsibility as parents is this: teach our children through our example to love God with all our heart; love God with all of our soul; love God with all of our might. Put God first in your life. If we as parents, through our example and our conversations with them throughout the day and night, if we communicate this to them, they will develop into true Christ followers. Talk to them about what they learned in their Church Bible Classes. Tell them how God is speaking to you personally. God is always doing something in your heart and life. If you're sensitive to it, then you can articulate it. He's constantly in touch with you, teaching, guiding and instructing you. We are to talk about those things with our children. Discuss these spiritual things with your children. As we do this our children are being taught all through the process.

I believe everything I've mentioned goes for our grandchildren too. Some of us have close relationships with our grandchildren. We have a wonderful opportunity and privilege to have input into their lives.

Move Out!

As the children are in our home, our relationship with them is that of teacher, trainer, disciplinarian and provider – it's all real hands-on stuff. You're a doctor sometimes, a nurse sometimes, and even a counselor on occasion. But as they grow up, and if you've done your job right, they eventually leave the home and go out and start contributing to society. (I read a statistic recently that states that you have more twenty and thirty year olds still living at home today than ever before in history.) A lot of them never leave because it's too good at home. Mom and dad provide for them. They've got food to eat, everything is there for them, and they have no rules. They can come and go as they want. Life is good for them. They have a place to stay that doesn't cost anything. You are giving them a ride on the gravy train. But as parents we are doing our children a great disservice when we don't teach them to grow up and go out on their own and be productive. We can help them financially to get started, but eventually it ought to be cut off so that you are not spending your life savings to raise your children – they can run you in debt and really hinder your future.   If we have taught them well, we will avoid getting those late night phone calls when the kids are in their twenties. "Dad, could you help me out? The lights are turned off at my house." It's one thing if they've been laid off or are out of work. It's another thing if they are mismanaging their money. It's quite another thing when they are not paying their bills but they are buying all kinds of new "toys".

Let me share with you what happens. We change from the parent who is real hands on, if we've taught them right, to the parent who is now their friend. We now take on the role of buddy, counselor, and advisor – as they need that. When they are growing up in your house, they maybe your friend, but I guarantee you there will be times that they will not think of you as their friend. If they don't have those thoughts occasionally, you're probably not doing a good job as a parent. There should be times when you're making life tough enough on them, because foolishness is bound up in the heart of a child. (Yes, it all comes full circle)

If we put the kids in the corner office and let them run the show, and we are not in the executive suite running operations, then those children will call the shots. They love to give orders and manipulate adults. Throw in the factor of a blended family and you have double trouble. It really becomes an important issue. Suddenly there are three or four parents to "turn to" when the other one is not making them happy. It needs to be a cohesive family unit that is running by the same set of rules and regulations on both ends.

Don't Do It *Again*

I gave you a list of don'ts. Let me give a few more. Don't overprotect your children. When you overprotect them, you shield them from the exposure they need in life. I'm not talking about exposure to hazardous waste or chemicals or the bad things in life. I'm talking about their need to fall off the bike a block away from home without you knowing about it. That's kid stuff. That's part of growing up. I'm all for safety but if I would have had a helmet for riding my bike, I can promise you that I would have made good use of said helmet.

Don't neglect your children. Don't get too busy in life. Don't discourage your children. You can accidentally discourage a child so easily. Avoid this at all cost. Be gentle on the amount of "miniscule" rules that you put in place. (What to eat, how to dress, where to sleep.) You do need rules, but it is easy to set too many rules in place. Pick and choose your battles. Your home can become a dull, boring place to be, with nothing but rules and regulations.

Don't be too busy.
"When we get too caught up in the busyness of the world, we lose connection with one another - and ourselves." — Jack Kornfield

Irreplaceable

Step-parents: never try to take the place of a biological parent. I performed a wedding for a couple and the new bride turned

to her step children and said, "I'm your new mother now."
You could see the consternation on the face of those children.
Their looks spoke volumes to everyone present. They were
essentially saying, "You are not my mother!" Here's the deal,
she could have gone soft for a while and given time for the
children to adjust to her. I don't think she meant to but she
actually pushed the issue. She was really excited for the kids,
but the kids didn't feel the excitement. Remember, if you're
the step parent, you will never replace the biological parent.
Don't try to. Be yourself in the relationship and just love their
socks off. Just love them. Be kind to them. Accept the
relationship for what it is. Don't try to make it something it's
not. Those children will eventually love you for who you are.
Don't try to make them call you mommy or daddy. Give that
some time. Let that happen. Like I told you earlier, we came
up with a name at our house: Laura was mammy. So my girls
still call her mammy today. My daughter loves me, but
sometimes she wants to talk to mammy. Be sensitive to those
things. Don't take it personal and give it time.

Here's some do's. I know this can't happen all of the time, but
if you can make this happen it's a good thing to sit down with
your ex-wife or ex-husband and go over some boundaries.
Plan to do an affirmation plan as much as you can. Now I
know you probably divorced because you couldn't get along.
There was probably a lot of immaturity, and mistakes made.
Going through a divorce causes a lot of bitter, hurtful things to
be said. A lot of times you think death would be easier than
divorce. Divorce is painful. I know divorce is tough, and I
know that conditions are not always perfect for you to get with
an ex and to negotiate. Sometimes there just isn't negotiation.
But if you can, I would recommend it to you because it can be
beneficial to your children. Even if you know in your heart
that the rules and regulations that you agree to with your ex
will probably not be followed, you will at least know in your
heart that you did the right thing: you spoke to them about it
and that you tried. You tried. That is really all that you can do
sometimes. But remember, your children are watching and
learning from you. Don't let them see you give up.

Never ever allow your children to bad mouth your ex. When you do, it teaches them something. Don't even allow it if the ex was in the wrong; in that I mean they did everything wrong, totally. When we allow our children to, or even worse, when we participate in bad mouthing the ex, we are really teaching them disrespect. We ought to say, "Look, there will come a day when I will talk to you about this issue, but right now, you honor your mother or you honor your father. We are not going to talk about them. We are not going to allow that in this home." That's the first step.

Let me tell you an even more important step. Do not allow ill words to leave their mouths towards your new spouse either; that is just huge. Don't allow them to talk badly about anyone, even if you are on their side in the situation. In front of the kids, you must have a united front with your mate. You are teaching something. If you'll follow this advice – (and this goes for couples who don't have the blended family as well) - keep a united front with your wife: when you have issues that you don't agree with, you and your spouse need to get alone and talk privately. Never argue in front of the children when it's not about the children. It's only ok to have disagreements in front of the children when it's not about the children. The children need to know that you are always going to be on the same page with each other.

I've heard people say, "My mom and dad never had a disagreement." Well, you maybe never saw them disagree. When you allow them to witness some disagreements it allows them to develop their confrontational skills. They are probably going to marry someone someday with whom they will have disagreements. They are going to say, "I never saw my mom and dad do this and I'm out of here." When you have some disagreements in front of them (and even if there's some intensity there) then they see that you fight and you make up; they see you kiss, and forgive one another after a disagreement. It will do them a world of good to hear those words, "You know what? I was wrong. I forgive you. I ask you to forgive me." Those are good things for our children to see and hear from us. That's real world stuff.

When you have the foundation of your life and marriage in Christ and His love, you have more than enough to forgive one another for whatever he/she does. If our marriage ever gets ruined, it will only be on my side of it, if she left. I know enough about her to know that she feels the same way. Because I'm going to forgive her for whatever and she's the same way with me. You know what that does? That creates trust in one another. I might get upset, I might get angry, we might have heated discussions, but at the end of the day I love her and she's forgiven.
We will work through the issues because we love each other. We are committed to our relationship.

The Evil Heart of a Child
Agree on the boundaries and the behavioral guidelines as much as possible. Understand this: your children are prone to test your boundaries. In a blended family, the tendency to test those boundaries are four-fold. Like I told you before, I have one child who has always pushed those boundaries. We'd say, "Don't touch that ornament" and then next thing you know, it's broken. Children are tempted to manipulate and to be in control if they can. They will control through biological parents, step parents, and they know no limitations. They will try to guilt you out. Yes, they will. They are smart little bundles of manipulative evilness! There are seasons of life that we all go through, and there is nothing like the blizzard that comes along with rebellious child! I'd like to say that we are all walking closely with God and He speaks to us every day. We wake up praying in the spirit every morning. But our little kids wake up with a sin nature every morning. Those little kids wake up with evil in their heart. That's why they need us. Some mornings I wake up and I don't feel saved. I need prayer too. I know that I am, and I have to make myself line up with what I know is right.

Commit yourself to emotional integrity. In the early years of our marriage, the emotional integrity commitment wasn't as strong as it is today. Out of our emotions comes our behavior. Our behavior is determined by our feelings. Our feelings and emotions come from our thought life. How we think determines how we feel and how we feel determines how we act. So, often times, in the beginning of a relationship, you spend time arguing about the craziest things. You've heard the age old stories of knock-down, drag-out fights over the toilet paper roll and the toothpaste tube. Most of us have a hundred percent failure rate in this area. I still don't get the order right at the fast food restaurant. And you know what? Somehow it's always my wife's order. I didn't get the right sauce to go with her nuggets or dressing for her salad. Seriously? How is it always her order? My wife says, "You know, you still struggle with this don't you?" I do. But see in the early days, I would get defensive. I'd say, "I told them right, they are all messed up." Sometimes they are messed up. But when I forget to order the little side items, it's my fault. In the early years, I'd come home with some Taco Bell and had the order so messed up. I was so frustrated. Frustrated with myself – I'd take that burrito and throw it against the counter. (Of course you've never done anything like that.) Refried beans wound up in the sink. Then I didn't have anything to eat.

You know, emotional integrity says this, "It's not worth it." Again, pick and choose your battles. You know what I do now? If we fight now it's totally different. Now if I get home and the order is still messed up, I say, "Op, I'm going back out." She says, "Oh, don't do that." I say, "No, I'm going!" She responds, "No! Stay home!" "No, I want to get this order right!" "No, please, stay home!" The whole discussion is totally reversed now. What do you want? No, what do *you* want? I want to please you. Well, I want to please *you*. Really, that's how it is. Emotional integrity is a big one.

It's Just a Thunderstorm

This next one is major. We have worked so hard on this one. In the early years of our marriage we were determined to make our house a house of peace. In every family, blended or not, you can have so much strife, bickering and arguing that no one wants to be there. Strife opens the door to the evil one. When you have a lot of bickering and strife between the parents and kids, you unknowingly create a spiritual atmosphere. The atmosphere you create is determines what is in the home. For example, I know this about clutter, messiness, and dirtiness; when you're in an environment where things are dirty, messy and cluttered, you're one step away from poverty coming into that home. You can create an atmosphere for poverty. You will find that all of a sudden you are financially depleted. The environment you created has allowed an avenue of poverty to come into the home. Poverty can be a spirit of lack.

Here's what else I know about strife in the home. The children have bad dreams. The parents have bad dreams. Fear is present in the home. People have to sleep with lights on all over the house. You hear every sound in the darkness of the night. A simple thunderstorm, a gift from God that nourishes the Earth, can turn a three year old into a blubbering mess who can't be consoled. Then Dad is tired and is like, "It's just a thunderstorm. Go back to sleep." Yeah, that works. Way to be deep and comforting to the sobbing and shivering little girl next to your bed.

Instead, it's okay to grab that little one, squeeze her lovingly, and say *"I've got you. I'm right here and I'm taking care of you. Everything is going to be all right. **Trust me**."* God is saying that to us during times of strife in our lives. We have to let him squeeze us. We have to trust him and have faith that everything really is going to be all right. So instead of focusing on the thunder, change your focus to the fact that a little strife can be a doorway to a moment with God.

I want to tell you strife also opens the door to sickness entering the home. James says, "For every evil work." Sickness is not of God. Sickness is of the evil one. Strife and constant bickering allows for more colds, flu and virus. It doesn't just mean because you have a cold, cough or allergy that you live in strife. I'm not saying that. But I am saying if the strife, bickering and put downs are constant, you'll notice that sickness finds its way into your home more frequently. It just seems like somebody is always sick in the home. It should not be that way.

Here's what I want you to know: if you don't agree with me, if you think I'm just crazy, I just want to challenge you to go to the Word of God on the subject of strife. See what strife does. It opens the door for every evil work in your home. Here's what you need to do, be quick to repent. Be quick to forgive. Forgive. Repent. Forgive. Repent. Be quick to do both of these. This will help you to become good at repenting and a good forgiver. I work on this in our home as well.

Dream A Little Dream With Me

It's one thing to teach your children to obey and make wise decisions, but I think you can bump it up a notch and begin to teach them to dream. Begin to teach your children to have a dream, a vision, and a goal for their life. Teach them how to use their faith to accomplish things. Teach them how to exercise their faith for healing, for that new bicycle, for that test at school and for daily needs. Teach them about sowing seed and expecting a harvest. Teach them by example. Let them be in on your faith projects too. We have a vision board at our house, and our children see what is current on our faith exercise. Now the day will come when we will attain some of the things on our board, and our children will have watched this and how we did it. It's seen before our eyes and it's the Word of God. We are talking about it and believing for it. It is such a moment to be cherished when something for which we've had faith comes to fruition. We have a celebration. We thank God. We are also being thankful for where we are when things haven't happened yet. We are content with where we are. We are content with what we've got. We are pleased with what we've got. We petition the Lord with thanksgiving and a grateful heart for what we have and where we are. But we bring our requests and make them know to Him.

By teaching our children to do that, we are teaching them to walk in faith. There are some things for which we've been believing God for; for over twenty years. We are beginning to see some of these things come about. It's as if nothing happened for years and years, but we didn't give up. We kept praying, confessing and believing and now we are seeing a breakthrough in so many areas of our life. It is so healthy for the children to see that.

Ephesians 3:12 *"In Him, through faith, we may approach God with freedom and confidence. I ask you therefore not to be discouraged because of my sufferings for Him, which are your glory."*

What Paul is saying is, "In Him, we don't approach Him with fear and trembling, we approach Him with boldness and confidence." We teach our children to believe God for their needs – to get good grades, to be admitted to a particular school, to make a special team, to score goals, to improve at something. Whatever it might be, we teach them to apply their faith to it. Also to each them to plant a seed for someone else for what they are believing. Wouldn't it be ridiculous for a farmer to expect a harvest without planting seed? What he will see at harvest time is nothing but weeds. Well, Pastor I don't have any seed. That's not what the Bible says. The Bible says, "He gives seed to the sower." All you have to do is make up your mind you're going to be a sower. When your harvest does come up, then you have more seed. Pull some back for the next harvest. Teach your children this Bible principle.

Time, Love and Tenderness

Here are a couple of more things. These are things that kids need from a father. Your children, dad, need your time and your touch. (Oh yeah, we said that once already) When you walk by your son, stop and pat him on the back. Touch him.

Affirm him. Some studies tell us that a baby's health is tied to our touch. You need to hug, wrestle with and touch your children. Touch their face. You are also touching their lives.

Our children also need our time.

Our children need our talk and our communication. We need to talk to them about what interests them and what interests you. Do you know you are planting something in your children when you talk to them about what interests you? When they grow up they will know more about you. You won't bore them. They will love you. Also ask them what they are interested in.

Our children also need our tenderness. In this area we need to overdose our children with love. They need our affection, our love and our acceptance. Sometimes we have to be tough with them, but ninety percent of the time we need to buffer that with tenderness.

Teach your children to be positive rather than negative. That's hard to do if you're a negative person. But, if they see you working on being positive, you'll be teaching them by example. Teach them through conversation. Being negative is always the path of least resistance. It's easy to always look at what's wrong. It's simple to complain. Do you know that my temptation, when I'm visiting a new church, is to see what's wrong with it? This is because I'm looking from a critical viewpoint to see the flaws. I look for the right and the good too. But if I'm not careful I go negative, looking for crevices, cracks, litter, chipped paint, rust, water marks, spot marks, and carpets lifted up. The thing I'm really big on is smell. If a church smells weird it just ruins everything. It's so easy to go south for me in this area. But we ought to go positive instead.

One of my favorite words is tenacity. We ought to teach our children to be tenacious. I want my life to be a life of tenacity. I want is said of me, 'that guy would never quit. He would never give up. He was the most tenacious person I've ever known.' I want to teach my children to never give up, never quit. We ought to be so strong in our belief that we just never give up believing, going and pursuing. I'm not quitting on my wife, my children or my church.

"The most difficult thing is the decision to act, the rest is merely tenacity. The fears are paper tigers. You can do anything you decide to do. You can act to change and control your life; and the procedure, the process is its own reward." -Amelia Earhart

Every single blended family I know has someone in the family that sabotages the family. Sometimes it's father-in-law, sometimes it's the mother-in-law; often times it's the ex-father-in-law or ex- mother-in-law. It may even seem the dog is out to sabotage the family. Not really, it is just that at times, it does seem that opposition to unity and peace comes from every direction. Sometimes it's the ex-husband or ex-wife. It might even be the children who are sabotaging the family. It can be one or many. It happens. So be tenacious, have boundaries and never give up. There are no overnight fixes. One of best things you can get a grip on is to learn that you cannot change another person. If you have an out-of -control ex, in-law or teenager, these are times that you just have to set up some boundaries. It sounds hard, but as a Christian you need to give some tough love. Protect with boundaries. "I love you and I forgive, but I don't have to be close to you." You may have to love at a distance. You have to protect your family.

CHAPTER 7
SEVENty Times Seven

How Can I Forgive You Again?

We live in a culture of blended families. When couples come together, for a first marriage, it can be very exciting and sweet. But when you come with other family members, it can throw some extra ingredients into the mix. If there are too many elements in the mix, things can start to leave a sour taste in your mouth. Be quick to forgive and try to look for the best quality that each person in your family might have. But for starters, forgive yourself. Learn to love yourself before you commit to loving someone else and everything that comes along with that love.

Let me share some insightful information about singles. Over ninety-seven percent of all singles will get married. Many of those singles will marry into a blended family. What I have to say will help benefit, you in your situation, whatever it may be.

Let's talk about singles. With singles, the cloud of romance becomes so intense that our common sense and our good judgment just goes right out the door. Romance causes everything to look rosy.
We're in love. Don't you hear the violins playing? Can you smell the flowers? All of a sudden common sense disappears.

Here's what I've noticed. Married couples oftentimes have singles anointing and the singles oftentimes have married peoples anointing. What am I talking about? I'm talking about sex. Let's talk about it. Married people aren't having much sex and single people are having a lot of it. It ought to be the other way around. Part of the problem is that churches are not talking about it. The married people ought to be having all the sex, and the single people ought to be having none.

I want to start by giving you list that will help you when you start to date. Now don't take this list with you on your very first date. You won't get a second date if you do. These are just good guidelines to think about when you are considering relationships. Some of you might think, "I'll never marry." That's ok, too. It's great to be happy being single.

Why do you want to get married? That's one of the first questions I ask couples. Most people never ask themselves that question. I think that people just grow up thinking that's what's expected. You grow up, you find someone, and you get married. People of a certain age should get married and settle down. The problem with that mentality is that you can head blindly into some preconceived notion about how a relationship should be without understanding what it will require from you or your partner. The proof of that is reflected in the statistics we see on divorce. You have to know why you want to be married.

I think that singles sometimes feel inferior as a person because they don't have someone. They feel like they are just half a person. Some singles feel they need someone to fix their life. Some say, "I need someone to take care of me." If that is the basis of your marriage, it probably won't last. My first question then is, "Why do you want to be married?"

I think we get a clue on marriage when we look at what the scriptures say.
Ephesians 2:4 NASB7 *But God, being rich in mercy, because of His great love with which He loved us...*

Why Should I Share?
If you want to get married, it should be that you want to share life's journey with someone else. You want to pour you love into another. It's not about what you are going to get from it. It's about what you bring to the marriage. It's about what you can give, not what can you get. Don't feel like you are not whole unless you have another person in your life. You are whole all by yourself. Just you and God make a whole being.

I preface that with Jesus, because nobody ever feels satisfied without Christ. Once you have Christ in your life, you are whole, just you and God. So if you want to get married, it's because there is a purpose for your marriage. You will be sharing life's journey with another.

The other scripture I want to share is in Genesis.

Genesis 1:27-28 NASB *God created man in His own image, in the image of God He created him; male and female He created them. 28 God blessed them; and God said to them, "Be fruitful and multiply, and fill the earth, and subdue it; and rule over the fish of the sea and over the birds of the sky and over every living thing that moves on the earth."*

God didn't need anything, but He wanted someone to pour His love, mercy, kindness, blessings and goodness upon. Then He tells us He created us male and female, in partnership with Him- to use the vast resources given us for His purpose, to serve God and man. That is the basis for the marriage covenant. It's partnership with a purpose. Keep that in mind.

The whole reason God gave us marriage is so that we could do more, accomplish more and multiply. There are several scriptures that talk about the power of multiplication in God's Kingdom.

Deuteronomy 32:30 NASB *"How could one chase a thousand, And two put ten thousand to flight.*

He's talking about the power of relationship and coming together. When we go into a relationship for selfish reasons, we miss God's best for us. Instead, adopt the mind-set, 'What can I add to your life?' 'How can I help you become more?' The by-product of giving that to a relationship is more success for you. That's the law of sowing and reaping playing out in relationships. Simply put, *be the partner you want.*

If you're single and you have a desire to be married, you need to first of all get yourself ready for marriage. Prepare yourself emotionally, mentally, and spiritually. Get ready for a healthy relationship.

The first thing you can do to prepare yourself is learn to be content in your present situation. You are a whole person, not a half person waiting for someone to complete you. You are complete as a single person. You are all God intended for you to be as a single person. That's good news. Enjoy being single. Philippians 4:12 NIV *"... I have learned the secret of being content in any and every   situation..."*

If you will prepare for marriage and think about what you're bringing to the table in a covenant relationship, marriage will be very fulfilling. If you marry because you feel deficient or incomplete you're going to be unhappy. Some say, "I know I could be happy if I were married." The truth is that marriage does not make you happy. You need to be happy and content with who you are. Marriage is just icing on the cake. It's a partnership of two lives coming together to do life with purpose in mind. There is so much more to life than setting on the couch and watching television, going to work, coming home and going on vacations. That is such a low level of life. God has more in store for you than that. You are worth more than just existing. So prepare yourself for marriage. LIVE. Don't just exist.

1 Corinthians 7:32-34 NIV *I would like you to be free from concern. An unmarried man is concerned about the Lord's affairs--how he can please the Lord. 33 But a married man is concerned about the affairs of this world--how he can please his wife-- 34 and his interests are divided. An unmarried woman or virgin is concerned about the Lord's affairs: Her aim is to be devoted to the Lord in both body and spirit. But a married woman is concerned about the affairs of this world-- how she can please her husband.*
Paul is not saying that marriage is bad. He is saying that you have to know this in your mind. Have you ever seen married men and women live as if they were single? You know what happens to those marriages. They don't last very long. Or one person who stays but is absolutely miserable. In a marriage relationship, there is give and take. You can't live like you're single and have all the benefits of marriage. Enter your

marriage with a heart of forgiveness because you will have to learn to do a lot of it. When you come together in partnership and you have your interests on the same page, serving God, you will succeed. God has a purpose for marriage, and it is way beyond any of our selfish interests. When you are married, you care deeply about what your husband or wife thinks. You care about spending time with your children. Paul isn't saying marriage is bad; he's saying, 'keep this in mind before you get married.' There will be energy you'll have to pour into that relationship. If you want a good marriage, this must be a priority. Remember, 'Happy wife, happy life.' It's true.

GOAL!

We oftentimes think we have to have love in order to be complete. Here's what you ought to do. Fall in love with yourself first. I have a blended family. I'm writing from experience. I went through a divorce. I was twenty-three years old. I got married very young. One of the things I learned after the divorce was that I had to learn to love myself. I learned that I've got enough love for me. I'm not deficient on love for me. So whenever I found Laura, I wasn't looking for her to complete me. Now if she wants to add to my love, then I say yes. That's great. But I'm not looking for love to come because I'm incomplete and deficient on my own.

Now let me share something with you that will move you into the top three percent of all the people in the world. Honestly, it can happen for you instantly if you get a hold of this. You will move into the top three percent of all the people who've ever been born. Would you like that?

Here it is. ***Write your goals down***. Did you know ninety-seven percent of all the people who've ever been born and are living today will never write their goals down? Write down a vision. Write down a dream. If you want some things out of a relationship, write down what it is you want. God is a dreamer. He's a planner. God has a dream and plan for your life. He wants you to succeed. He wants you to be tenacious.

Get yourself ready. Having goals and a vision may sound preachy, but it's fundamental to having a successful relationship. You may say, "Oh, I've heard this before." Well, I really want you to get this. This is vital. This IS the work. Your life will stay the same, out of sync, if you don't assimilate this. You've heard the definition of insanity – doing the same thing all your life and expecting a different result. Do you know you won't get a different result? Even if you got a different result one day, eventually you'd go right back into the same thing because you reap what you sow. That is why you have got to think about the future. You must begin to think vision. Think positive. Ask yourself, "What do I want from life?" Don't settle because God has someone for you.

Here's why it's important to have a dream and vision for your life: because God has a dream for your life. He has prepared a path for you to walk on. He has a plan and purpose for your life. Often times we don't know what that plan is. I can tell you this. When you fall in love with Him, and you start serving Him, He begins to reveal His plan for your life. This is one of my favorite scriptures:

Ephesians 2:10 NIV *For we are God's workmanship, created in Christ Jesus to do good works, which God prepared in advance for us to do.*

When I went through my divorce, I felt like I had missed every good thing that God had ever planned for me. I felt like I had missed what He had prearranged. But watch how good God is – even when we mess it up with our mistakes. God has a way when we get busy with His purpose for our life. He introduces us to the right person who happens to be on the right path also.

We need to get on God's path instead of having our eyes always focusing on this girl or that girl, or this guy or that guy. All of sudden, life will explode before you and bam, there she is or there he is. He or she is everything you've been looking for. And God knew it all along. You just had to trust Him. If I would have stayed home feeling sorry for myself, then I would have missed God's will. Had I gone to the bars, I would have missed the path He set for me. If I were not on the path, playing around with my life, trying to do it my way, then my wife and I would have never gotten together, because we met in church. I was on the right path. I was not perfect. I had made mistakes. I didn't get it right for a while, but I finally got it together. God was so good to me! When I got serious with God, He got serious with me. He brought me someone that has blessed my life so much. The most important decision I've ever made outside of surrendering my life to Christ was choosing to be a serious Christ follower. That's when I found my spouse.

God isn't going to bring someone wonderful into your life if your life isn't what it should be. You could mess their life up, too. God loves them enough not to do that to them. He won't do that to you or me.

Partake of the Elements

The covenant in marriage is much deeper than a contract. The covenant of marriage is God bringing two people together. There are three elements to a good marriage and a good relationship. Here are the three things. Number one is **diversity**. Have you ever heard, 'opposites attract?' They do attract. Remember this, **common direction**? It's number two. **Deliberate destination** is the third element. Now, if you only have the first one and you don't have the last two, you're going to fight.

Opposites attract, but unless you're going the same direction and have the same vision, you really have no reason to get along with each other. People change, looks change and attraction fades like a beautiful sunset. If you're going here and I'm going there, and we have two totally different agendas, all we are going to have is ongoing conflict. I like red, she likes blue. Opposites attract, and God puts you together with people who have strengths to cover your weaknesses. That's the diversity in the relationship. Your husband may be good with numbers, figures and book work. You may be horrible with money. But God puts partnerships together to accomplish something. When the two of you work together in your strengths, you accomplish things. So where I'm weak, she is strong, and where she is weak I'm strong. That's the opposites in personality coming together for a purpose to accomplish something. In my case, she is very organized. I am quite as organized. She helps him. I have a tendency to fill the calendar up every single minute of the day. She, often says to me "What about rest and relaxation? What about vacation? What about time with our kids?" Laura really helps me in these areas. I would run myself into the ground without her help.

God will accomplish His purpose when the two of you work together in unity – allowing your strengths to complement one another. That's where diversity is wonderful, but if you're not doing anything for God in your life – then when those strengths and weaknesses come together, all they do is butt heads and create strife. The relationship is most productive when we are diversified and different, when we complement one another without duplicating one another. I don't need another me and she doesn't need another like herself. We need each other. The thing that makes it work is that we are going the same direction. We have the same destination. Even through conflict, differences and diversity we are headed in the same direction. You have to stop along the way and ask, "How are we doing on the vision? Are we still on track for the goal? Are we still going in the same direction?"

If these questions aren't asked, then years can pass and you have two totally different agendas. You haven't talked about it, but you feel yourself pulling apart because you are now going in different directions. If God isn't the Lord of my life, then I'm in charge of my life. If I'm married to someone who doesn't know the Lord and has no compassion for the Kingdom, guess who the Lord of their life is? They are. You can't have one partner submitted to the living God and the other partner being self-centered with life revolving around them. That's why Jesus said, "Don't be yoked together with unbelievers."

How many marriages have we observed where one of the partners said, "Well, he/she is a Christian?" How does he/she live? Are they Christian in name only? Or are they a true Christ follower? Do you have to drag them to church? Is reading the Bible painful for them? Having the basic common goal and vision of following Christ is too important to leave to chance. Be sure.

Find someone who likes the same things you like. Look for someone who accepts and likes your friends. Do they like the same music that you like? What do you like to do for recreation? I've seen marriages fall apart simply because the husband loves sports, love to fish, and she totally hates it. She's not social. She doesn't like to be around people. She wants to stay home all the time. They start moving in different directions because they are basically misaligned. You're heard the old saying, "Couples that play together, stay together." But if one doesn't want to go anywhere the other wants to go, trouble is imminent. So, when looking for your perfect mate, find out their interests and what they like to do. And see if it's something you like, too.

CHAPTER 8
Eight is Enough

Can We Become Compatible?

When the pastor met with the bride-to-be concerning who would be in the wedding party, it went something like this:
The <u>bridesmaids</u>: let's see, there's my whole sister from my mom and dad, my half-sister from my mom's side, my half-sister from my dad's side, my step-sister from my step-moms side, my step-sister from my step-dad's side, my step, step-sister from my step-mom's ex-husbands side, and my step, step, step- sisters from my step-dad's wife's ex-husband's side – I think that does it.

The <u>groomsmen</u>:   that would be my five step-brothers and my fiancé's two half-brothers.

The <u>flower girl</u> and the <u>ring bearer</u>:   that would be my daughter from my previous marriage and my fiancées son from his previous marriage.

Of course we're talking about the blended family. Have you ever had a smoothie? Strawberry Banana is pretty good. Add a little Kale in for good health and things come together nicely. Then you throw in a pepper or an onion. What about some garlic? Wait a minute. Strawberries alone are great. Onions add a lot of flavor to a stir fry. But mixed together, that is one nasty smoothie. Strangely enough, some people like extreme taste.
Our blended relationships are very similar. A bunch of people come together in a blended relationship that should be good, it should be working. But oftentimes things turn bitter. Even in un-blended families things turn bitter. So what can we do?

Let's start with a few more pointers for singles; these points can also apply to married couples.

What do you look for in a mate?

The Bible says in 2 Corinthians 6:14, not to be yoked together with unbelievers. That is so basic. Amos says, "How can two walk together unless they be in agreement?" The Lord points this out to remind us that if we're believers and Jesus is the Lord of our life, we have a master that is beyond us. We're submitting to a higher power. We're not our own boss. If we're believers then we are lead by the Holy Spirit. That's a pretty awesome boss.

If a person is a nominal Christian, a Christian in name only (and not actually following Christ's teachings), then who is in charge of their life? They are. You get a person who is running their own life yoked up with a person who is surrendered to Christ, and you have a recipe for continuous conflict. You'll have different goals, visions, dreams and directions in life. The two of you are traveling different paths. The basic foundation for Christians is to come together with other Christians, to be part of the body of Christ.

On the other hand, don't look for perfection either. In Roman's 3:10, it says, *"There is no one righteous, not even one."* So I want to help you make a better choice. You don't make a life decision based on the potential change of another human being. That is ridiculous. It seems like women are prone to make this poor decision, especially young woman. They find someone who is good looking, has a great job, and is a real charmer. He has a sense of morality. He doesn't cheat on his taxes, he's a hard worker and everybody seems to like him. However, he is not a Christ follower. But because he's attracted to her, he is willing to go to church with her for a while. This is not good enough.

Somebody Save Me

If you go looking for a mate, then they should already be living life with Christ. They should already be on the same path you're on and headed in the same direction that you are. Women who are dating unbelievers often drag their dates to church. Reading the Bible for these men is painful. They just come to make an impression. If you think life is going to be good for you just because you marry someone good looking, or who has a good job, think again. If Jesus is not Lord of their life then you are in for a rough road. We all know people who've done this. These people pray and beg God to save their spouse.

Even if a person is a Christian, but they are not serving God, don't date them. They are deficient in their character. You're tempted to think that you can fix them. Don't count on it, because they may never change. Don't date projects. Don't think, 'Oh, I can change him/her.' That's a huge mistake. People with the gift of mercy often think they can nurse a person back to life. They want to adopt every little stray animal they see on the side of the road. They seem drawn to men or women who are needy people. They are always trying to fix somebody. They date someone thinking, "I can change them." Don't date projects, marriage is hard enough. God has to save them long before you can, in fact you can't save them at all.

It's not uncommon for a couple to come to me after six months of marriage. Often, the guy will say, "She's trying to change me. She's not happy with me anymore. She doesn't like me for who I am." This happens because during the dating relationship things are so romantic, mystical and flowery that we are willing to overlook everything. In the back of our minds we say, "Well, he'll change for me." Then, as soon as the ring goes on and they are married, she goes to work on him – to change him. Let me tell you that you can't change another person. You'll never be able to do it. Love them the way they are and know that they are probably not as good as they appear to be in your mind. First impressions are not always true impressions. Rarely are people as they first appear.

Sometimes they are better. Sometimes they are worse. Give time a chance. It has a way of bringing out the truth. There are things people won't tell you, even friends won't tell you, but time tells all. Take enough time to see the person for who they really are.

There was a woman I know who broke up with a guy she was dating over something very simple. With her it was a big red flag, and she took note of it. They went to a movie and the guy she was dating said, "Hey, I think we can sneak in this side door. I do this all time, and we won't have to pay." She didn't say anything, but that was her last date with him. She said, "I know that if he is willing to do that, and be so blatantly open about it, then he's a thief and a cheat. He's lacking in character and integrity. If he's willing to cheat in that situation, then there's a pretty good chance he's going to do that to me." So even in a dating relationship, the blinders need to come off. You really ought to inspect the prospect. After all, this is a lifetime investment, right?

However, when you get married, you need to put the blinders back on. You go into marriage with your eyes wide open. That's the time to notice everything. It's not the time to be clouded. This is why God says that sex is for the marriage covenant. So many young people get involve in a sexual relationship before they are ever really friends and before they are married. That clouds your judgment.

Sex is a gift from God to the husband and wife. It's not just to make babies. It's not just for procreation. The gift of sex, in the context of marriage, is for pleasure. What happens when you experience the full dimensions of your sexuality outside the marriage covenant is that a major cloud develops between you and God. You also fail to experience the true intimacy that God intended for a husband and wife. Marriage is a covenant, not a contract that is easily broken.

A Life and Death Situation

Covenant is a life and death union. If you understand covenant and you realize what you are entering into when you marry, you have a new mindset toward your marriage relationship. When you bypass the dating and courting aspect of your coming together as a couple, you miss major character deficiencies. The cloud of guilt that comes between you and God also clouds your ability to see the other person clearly. If you're single and you've been having sex, the good news is you can be forgiven. God will forgive you when you repent. Change your way of thinking about the issue and discontinue having sex outside of marriage.

You can tell a whole lot about a person that you're thinking about dating by looking at their friendships and relationships. Who are their friends? What are their characters like? How do they behave? Who do you like to hang out with? These are all valid questions.

1 Corinthians 15:33 NIV *Do not be misled: "Bad company corrupts good character." (It doesn't say it's the other way around.)* *34 Come back to your senses as you ought, and stop sinning; for there are some who are ignorant of God.*
We think we can hang out with people of character deficiencies and be okay because our good character will rub off on them. It just doesn't happen that way. You can influence people but you don't do that in a dating relationship. You can easily be blinded by a lustful eye.

Throughout this book I have led you in the direction that will help you as you enter or continue on your journey as a blended family. As a new spouse, remember to look for the positive things in your significant other and work together as a united force. Put God first and put each other first. If you already have children that you are bringing together, look to His word when you feel lost or distraught. Never sleep with anger or jealousy in your heart. As a parent and leader of your family, remember to lead by example. Practice what you preach. You are the scriptwriter that is dictating the actions of your children. They have been given to you as the most precious gift from God, both biological and step children. They are looking to you for a pure, steadfast heart. They see and learn so much more than you might ever suspect.

You should never marry someone with the attitude that they are a 'project.' If you think you'll bring God-like change into their life, you're deceiving yourself. My daughter, Cassidy who is now 7 at the time of this writing, came to me and said, "Dad, there's this boy in my class who said, he's my boyfriend. But I had to dump him." I said, "Why did you dump him?" She said, "He just does not respect girls."

Yep, that's my girl.

Genesis 2:18-24 ESV *Then the Lord God said, "It is not good that the man should be alone; I will make him a helper fit for him."*

Final Thought

Let me leave you with this one last thought. You can have a great marriage and a great family. You really can! I encourage you to stay the course, and don't grow weary. The effort it takes to have a great marriage and family is worth it. I am praying for you and your family today. I pray for every eye that reads these pages to be empowered and strengthened as you live and do life.

Marriage, family, children, parenting, career, business, life – blend it all together and it has the potential to be something incredible. The key is to keep the first things first. The order of the priorities in our lives determines the quality and the quantity of our lives.

I encourage you to put God first, then marriage, family, and career next. Also, a great question to ask yourself to keep your perspective healthy during times of difficulty is this: Will it really matter 100 years from now? If it won't, let it go.

Maintain an eternal perspective; your family and the relationships you have are the only thing you will be able to take with you into eternity.

Be encouraged! I believe in you!

May you be blessed and protected. May God make His face to shine upon you and show you His favor. May you live in His grace and mercy, experience His peace, and be filled with His joy and love. May you become contagious with that love and joy, and may you infect others with it. I declare you to be blessed!

Daren Carstens

About the Author

With a passion for life and a desire to help people reach their full potential, Daren Carstens is pastor of Enjoy Church, a multi-denominational, multi-campus church serving the greater St. Louis area. As an author, speaker, and mentor, Daren is the son of an often-travelling pastor and has a background in construction, retail, and leadership development. Daren mixes his humorous, encouraging, and energetic style with practical real-world experience, which has allowed him to reach thousands of people every week through the church's physical locations, an online campus, and weekly television programs.

Daren and his wife Laura have a blended family consisting of 5 children and 4 grandchildren. They are excited to share their experiences in order to help and support others with blended families.

You can find more information on Daren by viewing one of his social media pages or by visiting his church website.

www.facebook.com/DarenWCarstens
www.twitter.com/DarenCarstens
www.daren.tv
www.Enjoychurch.tv

Questions or Comments for the Author

Daren would love to hear your thoughts. Email at assistant@daren.tv

Would you like to receive my free newsletter?
Sign Up at www.daren.tv

View Other Books by Daren Carstens
Overcoming: Overwhelmed

Go to www.daren.tv

Request for speaking engagement
Contact: Request@daren.tv

Hear Daren Speak live online at
www.Enjoychurch.tv

One Last Thing...

Would you share your thoughts through your Facebook and Twitter accounts? If you believe your friends would get something valuable out of this book, or if you feel strongly about impact this book has made on your life, I would be honored if you would share your thoughts. I would be grateful to you if you would post a review on Facebook and Twitter.

All the best,

Daren

Made in the USA
Lexington, KY
12 January 2015